SOMETHING FOR NOTHING

SOMETHING FOR NOTHING

by Sid Roth
with
Irene Burk Harrell

Logos International
Plainfield, New Jersey

Scripture quotations are taken from *The Holy Scriptures, Revised in Accordance with Jewish Tradition and Modern Biblical Scholarship*, by Alexander Harkavy. New York: Hebrew Publishing Company, © 1936.

Quotations from *The Bible, the Supernatural, and the Jews*, by McCandlish Phillips are copyrighted 1970 by The Bethany Fellowship, Inc., Minneapolis, Minnesota, and are used by permission.

Italicized chapter headnotes are from *The Confessions* of *St. Augustine*, translated by F.J. Sheed. New York: Sheed and Ward, © 1943. Used by permission.

Library of Congress Catalog Card Number: 75-31396
International Standard Book Number: 0-88270-145-2 (cloth)
0-88270-146-0 (paper)
0-88270-258-0 (pocket)

To Joy

CONTENTS

For More Information
Call or Write
GOOD NEWS FOR ISRAEL
Box 23018
Richfield, MN 55423
(612) 881-2311

SOMETHING FOR NOTHING

You, Lord, . . . turned me back towards myself, taking me from behind my own back where I had put myself all the time that I preferred not to see myself. And You set me there before my own face that I might see how vile I was, how twisted and unclean and spotted and ulcerous. I saw myself and was horrified; but there was no way to flee from myself. If I tried to turn my gaze from myself, there . . . again You were setting me face to face with myself, forcing me upon my own sight, that I might see my iniquity and loathe it. I had known it, but I had pretended not to see it, had deliberately looked the other way and let it go from my mind.

Chapter 1

Death Sentence

My God! How had anyone been able to stand me? Why hadn't somebody killed me long before now? I didn't like the sudden blinding revelation that showed me to myself, the revelation that I, who had always thought I was so wonderful, was a total washout as a person. It sickened, it hurt, I wanted to deny it, but try as I might, I couldn't think of one justification for my life. There wasn't a single good, decent quality in me. Why was God letting me live?

Maybe He wasn't! The thought careened through my head, and I couldn't stop it. Maybe the flashing of my whole life before me was a prelude to its end—that very day.

1

But God! I'm not ready to die!

I drove aimlessly around the city for several hours,
going like an automaton through the mechanical motions of
stopping for traffic signals, changing lanes, accelerating,
slowing, thinking. . . .

As I considered the life I'd lived, really seeing myself
for the first time, the evil that was in me seemed to swell
larger and larger, until I feared I would burst with it. But
why? Why had I been like that? Why had I never seen it
until now? Was there any hope for me?

As the unanswerable questions swirled, I considered
crashing my car into the fast-moving traffic to wipe out the
awfulness of the past. But I was afraid. If I did that, maybe I
would land in hell, stuck with the awfulness that was myself
for an unending forever.

Unexplainably, I found myself parking in front of a big
bookstore I had frequented in the past. As I entered the
store, my feet took me automatically down the aisle to the
occult section. There, a book with a blue jacket leaped out
at me—*The Bible, the Supernatural, and the Jews* by
McCandlish Phillips. I reached for it, it fell open in my
hands, and I began to read:

> If you would not thrust your hand into a snake pit, you
> should not permit yourself to be drawn into an involve-
> ment with one or another form of occultism, even in a
> tentative and experimental way, without knowing that it
> is possible for you to step over a threshold and past a
> door that will slam shut behind you as soon as you stand
> on the far side of it—slam shut so tight that nothing you
> can do can ever get that door open again so that you can
> get back out.

Had the door already slammed shut on me because of
my involvement with horoscopes, fortune-telling, and
mind control? My heart was beating wildly as my eyes

skipped through the pages a little further. There I read something worse, something even more terrifying :

> The door that can never be opened again slams shut faster on a Jew than on a non-Jew.

The author went on to explain that this is true because every Jew, whether he knows it or not, is in a covenant relationship with God.

I felt beads of sweat popping out on my forehead. My throat was on fire. The gooseflesh of fear enveloped my whole body. But I couldn't put the book down.

I shoved some money across the counter to the check-out clerk and dashed back to my car, the book tightly clenched under my arm.

I wasn't even aware of driving to the apartment, just of suddenly arriving there, slamming out of the car, dashing through the lobby and into my room, torn with warring desires. Part of me wanted to devour the book, to read every word; another part of me wanted to rip it to shreds, to set it on fire—anything to get rid of it!

The page to which I opened named prominent Jews who had lost their lives because they had dabbled in the occult, opening the door to the supernatural through acid rock music, alcohol, marijuana, drugs, yoga, meditation, hypnotism, mind-expansion.

There was Brian Epstein, manager of the Beatles. Brian, a multimillionaire at thirty, was a Jew. He had dabbled in the occult, and he had died of an overdose of drugs. I shuddered, thinking how close I had come to following in his footsteps exactly. Phillips said that entering the supernatural world is like stepping across a manhole cover when you enter it, but when you want out, the cover is conve-

niently missing, and the only way out is straight down into
the very bowels of hell.

But I didn't want to die! I wasn't ready to die!

O God, help me! Somebody, help me!

Suddenly I knew that the devil was real, and that he
was personally in charge of every search for knowledge and
power that did not give the glory to God.

I had to get in touch with God! I had to tell Him how
sorry I was. For everything.

But I didn't know how to get in touch with God, and I
didn't know who could help me. My fortune-teller couldn't
help me. The mind control people couldn't help me. They
said there was no such thing as evil. My rabbi? He'd probably send me to a psychiatrist who would lock me up and
throw the key away. My mother couldn't help me. She
didn't know God either.

Panic stricken, I rushed out and ran to a jewelry store
in the neighborhood. There I bought a Jewish mezuzah and
hung it around my neck. Maybe that would show God that
I belonged to Him. I telephoned Joy, my estranged wife.

"Pray for me," I pleaded. "Pray like you've never
prayed before! Pray to your God for me! Ask Him to help
me. *Please* ask Him to help me. Ask Him to spare my life!"

I let the phone fall from my hand, weeping in an agony
of despair.

I could feel the fear building in me, a tangible thing,
building toward a crescendo. When the crash came—and
when it was over (would it ever be over? or was terror
eternal?)—where would I be? Or would there be anything
left of me to be anywhere?

A man under a death sentence, I put my Bible under
my pillow, felt of the mezuzah around my neck, and
crawled trembling into bed. Lying there on my back, rigid

with terror—I cried out, "O God of Abraham, Isaac, and Jacob, whoever You are, if You're listening, please, please help me. Get me out of the mess I'm in. I don't want to wake up, ever, if life has to be like this!"

It wasn't much of a prayer, but it came from a broken and contrite heart.

When I did not get what I wanted . . . I was in a rage—with my parents as though I had a right to their submission, with free human beings as though they had been bound to serve me; and I took my revenge in screams. . . . Surely it was not good, even for that time of life, to scream for things that would have been thoroughly bad for me; to fly into hot rage because older persons . . . were not obedient to me; to strike out as hard as I could, with sheer will to hurt, at my parents and other sensible folk for not yielding to demands which could only have been granted at my peril.

Chapter 2

King Me!

The train was crowded with well-dressed travelers going from Washington to New York for the holidays. Overhead racks were jammed with brightly wrapped packages and folded-up overcoats. All the seats were filled, and some extra passengers perched on their suitcases in the aisle. As the streamliner plowed its way through the snow-covered countryside, a small blond-headed boy wrestled himself loose from his father's restraining grasp and threw himself down in the aisle, screaming at the top of his lungs, beating his feet in a tantrum staccato against the green-carpeted floor of the passenger coach.

"Waaah! I'm starving! Waaah! I want a hamburger! Waaah! I want a hamburger! Waaah!"

There was almost a rhythm to it, punctuated by the rapid clicking of the train wheels along the track. The boy's father glowered ferociously and started to get up from his seat, but his wife's firm grip on his coattail pulled him down, her voice hypnotically persuasive.

"Be patient, Jack. After all, he's just a child. When he's older, then we can reason with him, teach him the difference between right and wrong. Right now, he probably *is* hungry. It's been a whole hour since lunch."

The man gave a deep sigh of resignation and pulled his coat close around him. Grunting what must have been an assent, he stared straight ahead. His wife rummaged in her capacious pocketbook and came up with a handful of shiny coins. Edging her way into the aisle, she knelt beside the still kicking, still screaming child.

"Here you are, Sidney," she purred, showing him the money. "Come with me, and I'll get the hamburger for you."

He stopped his wailing, looked as if he might begin all over again, and demanded suspiciously, "Can I have lots of ketchup on it?"

"A whole bottleful if you want it." The woman smiled at him, smoothing his hair and helping him to his feet. There seemed in her a vibrant pride and no shame at all that the coach full of passengers, who had been dozing, reading, or engaged in quiet conversation, had stopped what they were doing to stare at the almost unreal melodrama taking place before them.

But the scene was real enough for all of the three participants. They had been through many similar scenes in the past.

I was the temper-tantrum child, and my mother was the epitome of indulgence, my secret weapon against my father and anyone else in the world who didn't want to let me have my own way.

There are other scenes vivid in my memory even today. I can see myself running around our dining-room table, making "Nyah, nyah, nyah" faces at my father, in hot pursuit with his belt. But my secret weapon was always there between us, running interference for me, and I was never caught. I never felt the belt I so richly deserved. If I had, it might have made a difference in my life. It might have kept me from the day when, as a physically grown-up young man, I crawled into bed too terrified to close my eyes, but so scared of the mess I had made of my life that I thought it would be best for me to go to sleep and never wake up.

It was bad enough that my mother always pampered me in everything, but when I was four years old, much of the world joined her in letting me have my own way.

It all began when suddenly, for no reason that anyone could see, I started limping. I wasn't even aware of it myself until one night when there was a card party in our home. I had gone to bed early, sleeping as usual in my parents' bedroom. I woke up about midnight, as I had intended, in order to have some of the party refreshments. Rubbing the sleep out of my eyes, I stumbled into the living room in my rumpled pajamas.

"What's the matter with Sidney that he's limping so bad?" I heard someone ask my mother.

"Limping? My Sidney?" Mom was plainly startled. She slammed her handful of cards face down on the table and shoved her chair back, lines of real concern etched on her face.

"Aw, he's just faking, Ceal," my father said. "Come on, it's your bet. . . ."

But my mother had to find out right then what was wrong with her darling boy.

"Walk across the room to me, Sid," she pleaded, stretching out her arms.

I was happy to oblige, seeing that limping was a way of getting even more attention than usual. But I overdid the demonstration, walking with such an exaggerated limp, grimacing with such obviously fake pain on my face, that everyone except mom burst out laughing and turned their attention back to the game.

I consoled myself thinking of the food mom would be bringing out in just a little while. She made the best corned beef and pastrami sandwiches in the world, and she'd probably give me an extra one since everybody had laughed at me. I could always count on her to make things right.

In the days that followed, I continued to limp, even when I wasn't thinking about it. My father kept telling me to stop faking, but mom grew more and more concerned.

"Something's really wrong with Sidney, Jack," I heard her say to my father a few days later when he came home from his work as a government electrician.

"That limping business, you mean?" He squinted at me through the smoke curling up from his perpetually dangling cigarette. "Aw, the kid's just trying to get attention."

"Jack! I know it's something serious!" Mom yelled so loud that daddy didn't say anything more. He buried himself in the evening paper and she picked up the telephone to make an appointment with an orthopedic specialist.

There were lots of tests, x-rays and more x-rays. The diagnosis: Legg-Perthes disease of the right hip. The treatment: I would have to get the weight off my hip so it could heal.

"Poor Sidney," mom said, and the rest of the world demonstrated their sympathy, too.

At first I reveled in my new importance and the excitement of being fitted with crutches, braces, and a built-up shoe. Everyone showered me with gifts, and relatives and neighbors waited on me hand and foot. Even my father gave me everything I wanted for a while. When I went to the movies, someone would stand up to give me the best seat; when I entered the Halloween costume contest, I won first prize, not because my cowboy outfit was better than anyone else's, but because of my crutches. People who didn't know me thought that I was brave and wonderful. But their thinking it didn't make it so, and I grew fatter, sassier, and more spoiled than before. If there had been a contest about it, I could easily have won first prize for being the most obnoxious child in the world.

By the time I was old enough to be enrolled in kindergarten in the Hebrew Academy in Washington, D.C., I was sold on the idea that being crippled entitled me to everything I wanted from everybody. It must have been a real relief to my teachers when the doctors decided in January of my first-grade year that crutches and braces weren't doing the job. I was still putting too much weight on my hip, they said, and I would have to be taken out of school and hospitalized so my leg could be put in traction. That didn't sound too terrible to me, having my foot taped up and weights put on it. Besides, being in the hospital ought to be good for lots of presents!

In the hospital, I was challenged by a whole new group of people to bend to my way. But I soon learned that the nurses had had some experience in dealing with spoiled brats, and before long they demonstrated that they knew how to handle me.

A boy in the bed next to mine got to be my good friend, and we liked to trade our comic books and toys with one another. Since neither of us could get out of bed, we buzzed for the nurses continually and asked them to make the exchanges for us. One day, a nurse had had enough. She explained that she was very busy taking care of other patients and that we should not buzz for her again unless we really needed her. Naturally, after that, we buzzed twice as often as before. We didn't know that the nurse had a secret weapon of her own.

The next morning, two green-coated interns, their surgical masks dangling around their necks, came into our room, rolling a stretcher.

"Is this the kid to be operated on?" one asked the other, jerking his head in my direction.

The other intern nodded gravely. Unsmiling, they began to maneuver the stretcher close to my bed. Their exceedingly serious manner unnerved me. Maybe they were going to cut my leg off !

"No!" I screamed as loud as I could. "Not me! It's a terrible mistake! Call my mother! Call my mother!"

I rolled to the far side of my bed kicking and screaming louder and louder until the interns left the room, taking the stretcher with them.

I was too scared to buzz the nurses for anything else the rest of that day. When my mother came to see me before bedtime, I told her what had happened, embellishing the truth with all the gory fictional detail my imagination could dream up. She listened in horror, her eyebrows climbing higher and higher, first in shock, then in super-righteous indignation.

Armed with my account of incredible sadistic torture, mom rushed to the administrator's office and demanded that the two interns be fired, threatening a congressional investigation of the whole hospital staff.

I don't know what the administrator told her, but I do remember that I was transferred to a different hospital the next day. It was another case of my secret weapon at work, another case of my refusal to learn to behave in ways acceptable to the world.

When I was released from the second hospital, a visiting teacher came to my home to instruct me in what I had missed in school. Later, I was enrolled in a special health school with other handicapped children. By this time, I had been on crutches so long that I had recurring nightmares of frustration in which my hands were glued to the crutches. No matter how hard I waved my arms, I couldn't shake the crutches off. There was no way I could get rid of them. It was as if God was showing me, way back then, that I had cemented myself in a kind of life from which I could never rescue myself, no matter how hard I tried.

*I, poor wretch, could not see the use of the things I was
sent to school to learn . . . . I still did wrong, by writing or
reading or studying less than my set tasks. It was not, Lord,
that I lacked mind or memory, for You had given me as much
of these as my age required; but the one thing I reveled in was
play . . . .*

*I did not see the whirl of vileness into which I had been
cast away from Thy eyes: for what was more unclean than
I, seeing that I did not win the approval even of my own
kind: I told endless lies to my tutors, my masters, and my
parents. . . .*

*Even in games, when I was clearly outplayed, I tried to
win by cheating, from the vain desire for first place. At the
same time, I was indignant and argued furiously when I
caught anyone doing the very things that I had done to
others. When I was caught myself, I would fly into a rage
rather than give way.*

Chapter 3

Liar, Cheat

After I had spent three years in the health school, the
doctors were satisfied that I was healed of the Legg-Perthes
symptoms. They said I could discard my crutches and go to
a regular public school with normal children. I was so excited about not being a cripple anymore that I was *almost*
glad *not* to need special attention. But I got it anyway. My
mother saw to that. She told the teacher that I had been a
cripple, and the teacher explained it to the class and urged
the boys and girls to be extra patient and kind to me. For a
while, everyone cooperated, making it easy for me not to
grow up.

Eventually, after the school kids got over the novelty of the fact that I had been a cripple, they began to tease me about how fat I was, that I couldn't run very fast, and that I was making near-failing grades in school.

I coped with their criticism in my own way. "I'm not fat," I assured myself. "Mom always says I'm handsome, so I can't be too fat." Satisfied about that, I kept on stuffing myself continually.

I justified myself in physical education class by telling anyone who would listen, "Even though I've been on crutches for a long time, I can still run faster than so-and-so." (We had one *really* slow boy in our class.)

But even I had to admit that my grades were terrible. I had become so lazy in my study habits in the health school, where many of the children had low-normal IQs, I began to think that maybe I *was* dumb. But I never admitted that to anyone, and I persuaded my mother that it was the teachers and the school who were dumb, instead. The next year, mom put me in a private school where I would get more individual attention.

That didn't help. It actually made things worse. I was put in a class with poor and problem students, kids with learning disabilities. I was so far ahead of them at first that I just coasted for a while. By the time I realized that I was falling behind again, it was too late to catch up. Once again, I complained to my parents about what a stupid school I was in, and they put me back in public school the next year.

When things didn't go well for me in school, I was never reluctant to bring out my secret weapon. One day, a couple of boys teased me a little bit and shoved me. They were bigger and tougher than I was, so I didn't say anything at the time, but I vowed to get even with them. When I got home, I faked my way through a weepy scene with mom, telling her how two big bullies had beat me up.

The next morning, mom was at school, and the teacher let me stand at the front of the classroom and point out the culprits so they could be taken to the principal's office for discipline. Then mom passed out candy to the rest of the class, trying to buy their friendship for me.

Another time, I noticed that one of the boys in printing class had a better tray of print than I did. In my tray, the letters were all mixed up and I had to straighten them before I could set my type. In the other boy's tray, all the As were in the right compartment, all the Bs, and the rest of the alphabet was in order, too.

"It's because his brother went to school there," I whined, telling mom about it when I got home. "And his brother was so smart. That's why he got a better tray than me." She listened, full of sympathy, as always, and then she was on the phone, calling my classmate.

"You think you're so smart because your brother was a good student, and so you got the best tray, and my Sidney—" On and on she went, berating him, threatening him.

Sometimes I would be ashamed, but down deep inside, I must have wanted mom to keep on fighting my battles for me, because I kept on tattling to her every time anything went wrong.

I had so much trouble adjusting to people in life, that my mother finally sent me to a counselor to see if he could help me work out my problems with people. I went to see him a number of times before he finally gave up on me because I refused to admit that anything was wrong—with me. I told him that I didn't have any problems that I knew of. The problems were in the other people, I assured him. And so the problems continued, the battles grew more fierce.

My battles weren't confined to the schoolroom, either. One day I got into an argument with the son of one of our roomers, and I picked up a knife and held it to his throat . When he told his widowed mother about it, she consulted a lawyer. Then she made a bad mistake. She reported the incident to mom and told her that she was thinking of pressing charges against me. Mom's reaction was not at all what she expected.

"Out!" mom screamed at her. "Not tomorrow, not tonight, but right this minute!" The whole neighborhood could hear her screaming. "Out of this house, you and your good-for-nothing son. I'm looking at the clock! Out! Out! How dare you!"

Mom was screaming, and the poor widow was practically on her knees asking mom to forgive her, and asking me to forgive her and her son.

If there'd been an ounce of decency in me, I'd have felt sorry for them. But an ounce of decency, an iota of consideration for another human being, would have been lonesome in me.

In high school, I learned how to cheat in order to make the grades I wanted to have. I was good at cheating, and my eyes were always open to find new angles. One day in geometry class, I noticed that the teacher was copying our test onto the blackboard from a printed book of tests. Later that day, one of my friends told me that if I wanted to, I could probably buy a copy of the test book for myself with all the right answers printed in it! After school, I called the bookstore he suggested and sent my mother to buy the book for me. When she got home, I copied the answers for the next test we were supposed to have on a little slip of paper. At test time, I let it lie unobtrusively on the corner of my desk. I thought I was really cool to be writing the answers on my paper before the teacher even finished writing the problems on the board.

Even more fun than getting an A on the test was bragging to the other kids about how I was outsmarting the teacher. I thought I was outsmarting the teacher, too, when I let my friend Arnold copy my English homework every day for a whole semester. I thought we were getting by with it. But at the end of the semester, much to my surprise, the teacher held up before the class a couple of my homework papers and a couple of Arnold's.

"Isn't it interesting," she said, "that all semester long Sidney's papers and Arnold's have been identical? Now, Arnold and Sidney, I'm not going to ask who's cheating from whom. The one who copies work and the one who lets him copy it are both guilty. One's no better than the other." I could feel a sudden wave of heat spreading across my face, and I knew that even my ears were turning red with embarrassment. I shot Arnold a hate-filled look. *Why doesn't he at least tell her that he cheated from me?* I fumed. *The lousy cheat!* But I continued to cheat time and time again.

Once, I even cheated on a musical aptitude test!

I had studied, briefly, several instruments, such as the piano, drum, guitar, clarinet, and trumpet, but I didn't stick with any one instrument for more than a month, never long enough to learn anything. I was bored with having to spend time practicing scales and learning the rudiments. There was no glory, no public acclaim in that. I wanted to begin playing well immediately, and when I saw that mastering a particular instrument would take a lot of work, I dropped it and went on to something that looked easier.

When I was taking the aptitude test, I knew that the boy seated on my right had terrific musical ability, so I simply copied all his answers onto my paper.

When the test results were made known, my name was one of the two at the top of the list.

"These children have tremendous musical ability," the judge announced. I beamed back at him, adding another counterfeit star to my tarnished crown.

How I loved the glamor of recognition! How I despised the labor that led to real achievement! Somewhere, in the deep recesses of my being, there was beginning to stir an awareness that my deviousness might catch up with me some day, but I shoved the awareness down and kept on my selfish way.

Two goals for my life were beginning to crystallize in my thinking about this time. The first, to have the acclaim of the world; the second, to make a million dollars. I dedicated myself to doing whatever I had to do to achieve these goals.

To whom am I telling this? Not to Thee, O my God, but in Thy presence I am telling it to my own kind, to the race of men, or rather to that small part of the human race that may come upon these writings. And to what purpose do I tell it? Simply that I and any other who read may realize out of what depths we must cry to Thee.

Chapter 4

Hypocrite, Sluggard

I arrived at a major milestone in my journey to fame and wealth on September 7, 1953.

"Clothes really make the man, Sidney. You look absolutely handsome in your tuxedo." My mother sighed proudly as she pinned a fresh carnation to my lapel. She had on a long lace and chiffon dress, her shoulder weighted with an elaborate corsage. Everybody was dressed up. There were gifts, money, and parties in my honor. My head was spinning with the excitement of my bar mitzvah, the celebration of my thirteenth birthday, the day when a Jewish boy becomes a man.

I had been preparing for this day for five years under a

rabbi who was my special bar mitzvah instructor. I studied Hebrew, learned melodies to chant, memorized selections from my Haftaroth, and practiced the speech I would make in English.

The day was supposed to have real spiritual significance for me. It marked my coming of age as a son of the commandments. Now I was responsible for keeping them. But I don't remember even so much as thinking about God on that day. My thoughts were entirely of myself and *my* day, *my* appearance, *my* presents, *my* fun.

In my home, we had always observed all the Jewish holidays, usually making the trip to New York to spend them with my paternal grandparents. Those "vacations" had always been painful experiences for me. I disliked the long ride in the car or on a crowded train; climbing to the sixth floor of a tenement where there were no elevators; walking through the dark corridors that reeked with the stale aromas of food; boring hours sitting in the synagogue listening to a language I didn't understand; enduring interminable rituals that had no meaning or significance; all the relatives planting their sloppy kisses on me and asking stupid questions like, "How are you doing in school?" and "Sidney, you remember your uncle so-and-so?"

At these tribal gatherings, my parents were always bugging me. "Sidney, shake hands with your cousin. Sidney, did you say hello?" I always said hello, but I said it so softly that no one could hear me, and daddy would keep after me, growing more and more exasperated, "Sidney, you didn't say hello!" Today, as I look back, I know that my father loved me and was only trying to bring me up right, but at that time, I took a perverse kind of delight in provoking him to the verge of apoplexy.

In the midst of the frustration, there were a few fun

things I looked forward to—the seltzer water that sprayed from a nozzle, the matzo ball soup, the potato kugel, and getting a reward for the return of the matzo.

Stealing the piece of matzo, the unleavened bread, from under the pillow my grandfather sat on was my important part of the Passover seder, and the ceremony could not end until the matzo was back in grandfather's possession. It was part of the tradition that I was expected to demand a sum of money or a gift for its return.

One year, I fell asleep while the Passover seder was still going on. The prayers and Scripture readings always lasted for hours. Toward the end, my Uncle Willie woke me and handed me the matzo he had stolen for me. As I was thinking what gift I should ask for, or how much money I should demand, I made the smart-aleck mistake of waving the piece of matzo in front of my grandfather's face. With lightning speed, he grabbed it from my hand. I learned a new rule that holiday: never wave the matzo close to grandfather.

Although I didn't like everything about the holidays, and understood very little of their real significance, I was somehow, strangely, proud of my Jewishness. I knew I was born a Jew, would die a Jew, and knew with a fierce certainty that I would fight anyone who made fun of the Jews.

But attendance at the synagogue was another matter entirely. The only reason I went to the orthodox synagogue with my father was because I had to. The form of worship left me cold. There wasn't anything I liked about it except when we had refreshments.

I believed that there was a God, but the rabbi described God as a fire. What good could that kind of a God do for me?

It was all irrelevant, distant, and abstract. I couldn't

understand Hebrew, and the cantor's chanting was totally meaningless to me. Besides all that, the hypocrisy really got to me.

For instance, we would always park our car two blocks from the synagogue so no one would know that we drove on the holidays. But most of the others parked there too, for the same reason. Once I happened to wave the car keys in the synagogue. My father's look almost drove me through the floor. I had utterly disgraced him.

Another time, my yarmulke, my little skull cap, fell off my head in the synagogue and onto the floor. I hadn't noticed it, but my father had.

"Where's the yarmulke?" he growled at me.

I put my hand to my head, felt that the cap was gone, and reached down to pick it up off the floor. My father was almost sick with disgust at me for having my head uncovered in the synagogue. A friend who was standing on the other side of him tried to calm him down.

"It's all right, Jack," he said, putting his hand on dad's shoulder. "So the boy made a little mistake. Leave him alone already." I was so nervous I could hardly get my yarmulke back in place. Was it really such a sin to have my head uncovered?

And why did my relatives and friends smoke on high holy days when we were a block away from the synagogue where no one could see them, and then, when they got to the synagogue, why did they pretend they were abstaining from smoking? On high holy days, no one was supposed to light a fire for any purpose, because lighting a fire is work.

Why all the hypocrisy? Why?

I used to ask people about some of these things that bothered me, but everyone shrugged their shoulders and said nothing, as if they didn't know either. No one ever gave me a real answer.

The hypocrisy I observed in some orthodox Jews, the radical inconsistency between what they taught and how they lived, probably helped me to rationalize the dishonesty and the hypocrisy in my own life.

After my bar mitzvah, I didn't attend the synagogue anymore—except on holidays—until much later when I found out what the synagogue was really all about. But that was after I had been to hell and back.

My very first job on my way to winning the acclaim of the world and making a million dollars was as a paperboy in our neighborhood.

When I was in junior high, it seemed that almost every newspaper I picked up had a front-page picture of a paperboy grinning out at me. The write-up would tell how great they were, and paperboys were always winning prizes and going on trips to exciting places. Another definite drawing card, as far as I was concerned, was a promotional scheme in which, for every new subscriber, paperboys were given coupons redeemable with the Good Humor man. The thought of free ice cream treats was an irresistible come-on, and I teased my parents until they agreed to sign the official documents that embarked me on my first business enterprise.

I delivered papers proudly for a few days, and got my parents, an uncle, and a few close neighbors as new subscribers. Then I woke up to a morning when it was pouring rain outside. I was so cozy and warm in bed, that instead of getting up to deliver the papers in the rain, I manufactured a sudden terrible cold, coughing so violently that my mother and sister brought me cough syrup and a hot-water bottle and insisted on delivering my papers for me while I stayed in bed and read the comic strips. That was so enjoyable that I had many fake sick days after that, days when it was sunny as well as when it rained, and the papers got delivered by my mom and my sister Shirley. If they ever caught on to my game, they never mentioned it. I, of course, was the one who got to pocket the profits.

After I got too big and important to work as a mere paper boy, I went to work running errands for my Uncle Sol, who owned a watch repair shop. I liked my uncle and thought it would be fun going to drug stores and variety stores that took in watches to repair, delivering them to my uncle so he could fix them, and then taking them back to the stores again.

For two weeks, I got along fine. I enjoyed the prestige of carrying valuable merchandise around the city. But late one afternoon, when there were no pickups to be made, no watches ready for delivery, my uncle handed me a can of scouring powder and a rag.

"Here, Sidney," he said, "the washroom sink looks terrible today. Give it a good scouring for me."

I couldn't believe my ears. Me? Scour a sink? I looked at the grimy sink, appalled that he would ask me to do such a menial, low-grade job. Why, anybody could clean a sink. It was beneath my dignity as a messenger delivering expensive watches to think of doing such a dirty chore.

I halfheartedly sprinkled some of the green powder onto the greasy film in the sink, rubbed it around a little with the rag, ran clean water to rinse it out, and gingerly dropped the gritty, soggy rag onto the crumpled paper towels in the wastebasket underneath the sink. Then I sat down on a high stool at the rear of the shop to nibble on peanuts and read the supply of comic books I had brought to the store to keep me occupied while I was waiting to run the next delivery.

I hadn't turned the first page before I heard my uncle bellowing out at me.

"Sidney! Come back here! You call this sink clean?"

"It looks clean to me," I lied, looking at how smudgy and gritty I had left it.

"Well, you need to have your eyes examined, then," he said, handing me the can of scouring powder again. "Now get your rag and clean it right, this time."

It nearly killed me to fish that nasty rag out of the wastebasket and scour the sink again. I don't think I did a much better job the second time, but I knew it would be the last time I'd ever have to clean *that* sink. It was almost five o'clock, and when five o'clock came, I would head for home and never go back to that job. I never did, either. The nerve of Uncle Sol, expecting *me* to clean a sink!

In my first two jobs, I had set a pattern that would last me for a good long time, letting someone else take over for me when the going was rough, not stooping to do what was required of me, taking only the best parts, the fun parts, the acclaim, for myself and leaving the drudgery, the cleanup, for someone else.

I loved the vanity of victory, and I loved too to have my ears tickled with the fictions of the theatre which set them to itching ever more burningly. . . . Those who put on such shows are held in high esteem. . . .

Nothing is utterly condemnable save vice: yet I grew in vice through desire of praise; and when I lacked opportunity to equal others in vice, I invented things I had not done, lest I might be held cowardly for being innocent, or contemptible for being chaste.

Chapter 5

Dead Center

I began really moving up in the world in my own estimation when I started palling around with Johnny Spitzberg. Johnny was a couple of years older than I was, but I had known him all my life, because his mother and mine were best friends. Johnny was everything I wasn't. He was a fantastic dancer, a skilled athlete, and he had a reputation for being good with women. Johnny belonged to the Wilner branch of AZA, a Jewish fraternity in our high school, and he told me he could get me in, too. I wanted to join, because I thought that would automatically mean I'd have some friends, I'd be popular, and naturally, I'd be invited to all the AZA parties.

At the first meeting to which I was invited, I had to

29

stand in the middle of a circle of members while they asked
me a lot of questions. I tried to give dignified, man-of-
the-world answers, especially to the question about why I
wanted to join Wilner. I rattled off some high-sounding
stuff about how such high caliber kids belonged, that I
wanted to associate with them, and that I hoped to contribute something to the organization. It was a snow job, but
they seemed pleased at my answers. I noticed a couple of
them polishing their fingernails on their shoulders, being
cocky and pleased with themselves. Their smiles made me
think they were pleased with me, too, and as my confidence grew, my defenses let down, so I was not prepared
for the next question. When they asked, "What do you
think of girls?" I didn't prepare a suave, smooth, sharp
answer for them. I just said, with sophomoric naivete, "Aw,
they're all right."

The whole room burst into uproarious laughter, and I
blushed a billion shades of red and purple. It really seemed
to break them up, but I was accepted into the club anyway.

Thinking about how they had laughed at my answer, I
wondered if maybe, just maybe, I would go into show business as a comedian like my uncle, Jay Jason, who had
worked the nightclub circuit.

I had a chance to try out my acting ability when I went
to my first AZA convention in Richmond. There we played
poker, told dirty jokes, and some of the kids got drunk. I
was a little high myself, relaxed enough not to be self-
conscious, and I really put on an act, pretending that I was
dead drunk, staggering down the stairs, muttering hilari-
ously stupid remarks, and falling all over myself. My new
friends talked for a long time afterward about how perfectly
crazy I was when I was drunk in Richmond, and I knew I
was on my way.

AZA continued to provide a kind of security and sense of accomplishment for me during the rest of high school. I wrote a humorous skit that was a big success, and eventually I became an officer in the chapter. The first tastes of success instead of failure in my life made me resolve that I would make up for my poor showing in high school by really making it in college.

During the summer between my graduation from high school and my first year at American University, I stayed with my grandmother in Atlantic City and worked on the boardwalk as a pitchman for a handwriting analysis booth. There I learned that I was good at persuading people to shell out their money. My budding confidence made me act so grown-up, so sure of myself, that I was actually approached by a prostitute one night. I walked away from her, my knees shaking, but I didn't fail to tell my friends all the details, embroidered with my fertile imagination.

It was clear to me from the bug-eyed way they listened, that I was really coming up in their estimation. One of them told me privately later, "You know, Sid, you used to be about the biggest klutz in town. But you've changed somehow. Now you act more like just one of the guys." He was so impressed, I knew he would be spreading the word around. Since I had arrived in his eyes, I had arrived in my own eyes, too.

All of a sudden, food began to take a back seat in my life. After all, there were more interesting things to do than just stuff myself all the time. There were parties, and girls, and all sorts of extracurricular activities. It was a brand-new world, but I was still in the dead-center of it.

As I sat waiting for my first job interview in the placement office of American University, I looked over some of the letters of recommendation in my dossier.

The first one, from the Dean of Students, read,

> Mr. Roth is a serious, pleasant, and sincere young man.
> He has a friendly disposition and a courteous reserved
> manner. He is well above the average in scholastic abil-
> ity and intelligence. He is stable and reliable . . . has
> high standards of ethics and adheres to strong moral
> principles. He is recommended highly for any position
> for which he is professionally or technically qualified.

The next letter, from one of my professors, said,

> Sidney has been a student in my classes in which he did
> excellent work. I have also had occasion to work with
> him in student organizations in which he was always to
> be counted on to do a fine job in every way. He has am-
> bition, takes pride in his work, and will be successful at
> whatever he attempts. I recommend him highly.

Another said,

> He has taken a leadership position on campus and is
> well-respected by his fellow students as well as by his
> teachers.

As I read over these references, pride oozed from my
every pore. I patted myself on the back that I had come a
long way from the mamma's baby high school fatso who
couldn't even make a decent grade without cheating, who
couldn't fend for himself in any conflict. Now, here I was,
slim, popular, about to be a university graduate with a
major in public relations. The world lay waiting at my feet.

I had chosen public relations for my major when I was
a freshman, hardly knowing what the subject meant, just
because someone told me it was an easy major. Neverthe-
less, it had proved to be the right one for me. My own public relations had soared, my name had been on the Dean's

honor roll, I had been president of a large campus organization, my social life was top-drawer, and my parents had bought me a new Chevy convertible as a reward for my good grades. On top of everything else, I had won the coveted Glover Leadership Scholarship in my senior year.

I stood at least ten feet tall when the receptionist called my name and I strode into the office for my job interview with a man from the New York Port Authority. I was wearing a brand-new suit, shoes shined to perfection, a Florida tan acquired during the recent semester break, and I was carrying those terrific references under my arm. The job was a difficult one to obtain, I had been told, but I was positive it was mine if I wanted it.

Later, the vocational counselor broke the news to me.

"You didn't get the job, Sid. Tough, man. The Port Authority representative said you acted like you thought the world owed you a living. He said you'd probably have two or three jobs before you'd realize the world doesn't revolve around you."

It stung, but I was aware that the vocational counselor was looking at me closely, to see how I would take it, so I just gave a disgusted snort at *their* stupidity and walked out.

What the Port Authority man had said would prove to be the understatement of the century. However, it didn't take long for me to discount it entirely, deciding he had some kind of a hang-up. He was probably jealous that I was so young and "with it," while he was on his way down and out the back door. He'd probably give the job to some old dodo, I rationalized, just so *he* could keep on feeling superior, polishing up his sick ego. That I was utterly consumed with polishing mine was hidden from my eyes. I was Mister It.

After I had fully rationalized my way out of my failure to get the job with the Port Authority, my self-confidence swelled up bigger than ever, and I landed a job doing PR work for a department-store chain in Rochester, New York. I said good-bye to my family and was off to make my million and conquer the world.

For a few weeks, I did well at my job. But then a supervisor came down to Rochester, just to see how things were going. We were in the midst of a rush promotion, and everyone in the office had been asked to help assemble and staple materials for distribution.

The biggest wheels in the office were manning staplers without complaint, even my boss and my boss's boss, just to get the job done. But I wasn't interested in sticking with something that dull, and after assembling a few packets, I went back to my desk and found something more interesting to occupy my valuable time.

The next week, my supervisor called me into his office. There were no preliminaries.

"Sid, remember when everybody except you was stapling promotional packets last week?"

"Yes," I acknowledged, wondering what was coming next.

"Well," he went on, "I hate to do this, but you really asked for it. I've been instructed to terminate you."

Unlike me, my supervisor was a man who believed in following his instructions.

My indignation flared. It was the case of the workroom sink all over again. He learned that I considered stapling *anything* to be a menial chore, far beneath my ability. After all, I was Sid Roth, one of the top grads of American University, with all those great credentials! And they expected me to staple things together? Any crummy kid with no education at all could do that!

Before I could quit, I was fired. The Rochester department store had no place for a man with my attitude. My first career job had lasted almost two months.

What was it the Port Authority man had said? That I would have two or three jobs before I realized the world didn't revolve around me? Ha! I'd show them.

When I returned home, I pretended that I had resigned my job in order to further my education by attending law school at George Washington University.

I didn't really want to go to law school, but I had to save face somehow, and this seemed as good a way as any. Besides, from what I had observed, lawyers were always right in the midst of everything having to do with money. Maybe my first million would come as Sid Roth, Attorney-at-Law.

My father was delighted. He took me to one of the finest stores in the city and bought me four new suits— conservative solid colors and pin stripes with vests—exactly what the most well-heeled young lawyer would wear. I looked the picture of success. My father went around bragging to everyone about how well I had done in the University, and how I was now on my way to becoming a rich and successful attorney.

But there was a flag on the play.

In college, I had found that there was nothing I couldn't learn if I worked hard, but in law school, although I was keeping up with my assignments, some of the professors were losing me completely because there were no shortcuts. I could see the handwriting on the wall. Not wanting to flunk out, I just quit going to class. I didn't bother to notify the school of my intentions, although I realized that early notification was necessary if I wanted a refund. After all, why should *I* worry? It wasn't my money, it belonged to my parents. They had paid for everything.

After mom realized I'd quit school, she telephoned the business office and asked them to give her a tuition refund, but it was too late. The refund deadline had passed. I took all my expensive, brand-new law books and sold them at a secondhand bookstore for next to nothing, thinking that they had been an awful waste of money. A pity. I was only glad it was my parents' money and not mine.

I was all hot for honours, money, marriage; and You made mock of my hotness. In my pursuit of these, I suffered most bitter disappointments, but in this You were good to me since I was thus prevented from taking delight in anything not Yourself.

Chapter 6

Big Deal

I wanted to get into something more exciting than school, something with glamor in it. The most exciting career I could think of was show business. I had spent several summers during college vacation chauffeuring my comedian uncle, Jay Jason, from one engagement to another at resorts in the Catskill Mountains. Show business had gotten into my blood then. I had also done a little songwriting and produced a couple of records during my college years. And there was my acclaimed drunk imitation in high school. Maybe show business was where I belonged.

I went to New Jersey to see my uncle and asked him if he could help me get started.

"Yeah, sure, Sid," he said, eager to help me get going. "You don't have any talent of your own, to speak of, but you're a born promoter. And you have your public relations degree. Why don't you go into the talent-scout business? I know a guy who could use an extra leg man. There wouldn't be any money in it at first, but he could show you the ropes."

He introduced me to Miles Millard, and I was off and running, sunglasses and all, looking more like Hollywood than the people who lived there.

For the first two months, I didn't do much except type contracts, listen to the negotiations between performers and Miles Millard, and ride the subways delivering official-looking papers here and there. It wasn't really too different from my old job of delivering watches for my Uncle Sol, but it looked big-time. I was staying with my uncle, so I didn't need much money, and I was promised a percentage of the contract for any new talent I brought into the agency.

I went everywhere looking for unrecognized talent, dreaming that I would "discover" an Elvis Presley and make, not one million, but several million, in short order. I could taste success. But where was the talent? I couldn't find any worth promoting.

And then, one rainy Friday afternoon, it happened. Nothing much had been going on, and we were about to lock up and call it a day when the impossible dream walked in. He was an obviously talented, terrifically good-looking young singer whose star was on the rise, and he was actually *looking* for an agency to represent him. His contract was owned by some relatives of his who were gangsters.

They paid his expenses, gave him a salary, and collected the rest of the take for themselves. That worked pretty well while he was an unknown, but now he was moving up so fast, they needed a legitimate front for him, an on-the-level recognized agency to represent him while they stayed in the background. He'd get to the top quicker, that way. We all agreed that the top was where he was destined to go.

The gangsters didn't want to come to our office to work out the details of how we would represent the boy, but they invited me to come to dinner at their place the next evening so we could come to a firm agreement and sign contracts all around.

Miles and I sat up half the night getting the papers ready. It was cloak and dagger all the way. I wasn't told where to come. A couple members of the gang picked me and Jim Brody up. Jim was a public relations man, too, a friend of mine who just happened to be in the office that afternoon. They invited him to come along. We drove through dark alleys I'd never seen before, and stopped in front of a dingy dry-cleaning shop on a rubbish-littered side street. The shop was closed, but one of the men had a key that let us in. Bells on the door set up a crazy clanging as it swung open, and I nearly jumped out of my skin. I didn't feel nearly as cool, confident, and master of the situation as I thought my clothes and oversized dark glasses made me look.

After we had brushed our way past rows and rows of rack-hung clothes, almost overpowering me with the smell of dry-cleaning fluid, we emerged into a bright and crowded kitchen where half a dozen guys were yelling at one another, stirring spaghetti in a huge pot, and gesticulating wildly.

I nodded curtly at everyone, kept my dark glasses on,

my eyes and ears open, and my mouth shut. I could see there was no point in trying to talk business until things had calmed down a little.

When the spaghetti was cooked, someone shoved a chair at me, and we all sat down at the big kitchen table with red plaid oilcloth on it. Books, papers, vases of flowers, cigar boxes, a sewing kit, and other paraphernalia of family living were shoved out of the way to make room for great platters full of steaming spaghetti piled high with succulent meatballs and tomato sauce, the most delicious I had ever eaten. There were even elegantly huge white linen napkins to be tucked around our necks.

Bending over the spaghetti and the hot bread that was crusty on the outside, steaming soft on the inside, I momentarily forgot the reason for my visit. Eventually, however, all the plates were empty, and chairs were tipped back from the table. Cigars were passed, more coffee was poured, and I was introduced to everybody as a representative of the talent office that was going to handle their singer.

Very businesslike, I opened my attache case and began to pull out the various forms I needed to present to them for discussion and their signatures to make the deal official. Before I had finished extracting the papers, however, Jim Brody opened his mouth and began to talk. My mouth fell open, too, in astonishment at what I heard coming out of his.

"You know," he said, in a confidential tone that indicated he was doing them a very great favor, "you guys shouldn't let that Miles Millard Agency represent the kid. Why, that Millard is incredibly cheap. He has more talent leaving him than he has coming in. Everybody's getting disgusted about what a lousy promoter he is. Nobody gets to the top once they sign with him."

Jim paused, scowled thoughtfully at his cigar for a breathless moment, and then delivered the final pronouncement: "A Millard contract is the quickest way to the bottom of the ladder, and any fool ought to be able to get to the bottom easy enough all by himself without paying Millard a percentage to help him tumble down." He finally stopped talking to laugh long and hard about what a cheapskate my boss was. After a few seconds of looking quizzically at one another, the tension broke, and everyone began to guffaw right along with him. One of them doubled over in merriment, so relieved that they hadn't made the mistake of signing with the outfit I represented.

I just sat there, trembling, the papers in my hands. I was too dumbfounded to know what to say. Trouble was, I knew Brody was right. We *didn't* have any good talent left in our agency. The truth was, we probably *would* run their singer straight into the ground, too.

When they had laughed themselves out, the gangsters all turned toward Brody with their questions.

"Yeah? Tell us more about all that? Can you prove it? Like for instance, who's leaving the agency now? And what outfit do you think we should sign up with?"

Jim had all the right answers for them; they believed him. Nobody asked me a thing. I was ignored just as completely as if I hadn't even been there.

I was glad no one was looking. It was impossible to keep the pain from showing on my face. I knew that everything Jim was saying was true; it had been true from the beginning, from the time I first went to work with Miles to learn the business. But I had kept telling myself that once we found a really great piece of talent, things would be different. And now I saw all my dreams—of traveling with the kid, staying at swanky Miami hotels, wining and dining with the biggest names in show business—disappearing down the drain. My grandiose plans for spending my millions were all kaput. Worse than that, no one even offered to take me home. I let myself out on the side street and walked for blocks to the subway, then took the long, late, bus ride to Teaneck, New Jersey, where my uncle lived. When I finally reached his house, I peeled off my beautiful suit and fell into bed, bone-weary and utterly discouraged, at the bottom of the world.

The next day, my former PR friend came by the office and clapped his hand on my shoulder before I could move out of his reach.

"Sid," he said, "you know, you're really a basically nice guy. You don't belong in this business. You don't know how rough these syndicate people can play. By fouling up the deal for you last night, I really did you a big favor— because I like you."

Friendship like that, I could do without. I didn't have to say a word. He read it in my face. And I never saw him again. Miles Millard didn't seem too upset. "Win a few, lose a few," he said when I told him how Brody had stolen the show at the dinner party. But he didn't urge me to stay on with his firm when I told him I thought it was time for me to head back to D.C. I had wasted three months, not even being able to support myself, let alone earning a million dollars. There was no future for me or anybody else in working with Miles Millard's talent agency. There must be the right job for me somewhere else, just waiting for me to come along.

Alas, by what stages was I brought down to the deepest depths of the pit, giving myself needless labour and turmoil of spirit for want of the truth: in that I sought You my God – to You I confess it, for You had pity on me even when I had not yet confessed – in that I sought You not according to the understanding of the mind by which You have set us above the beasts, but according to the sense of the flesh. Yet all the time You were more inward than the most inward place of my heart and loftier than the highest.

Chapter 7

Mr. Cool

I went back home to live with my parents again. That was hard after tasting independence from their interference while I was living in New Jersey. But I settled in and went to work for my watch repairman Uncle Sol again, this time as sales manager for his more than 100 retail pick-up locations. It was a stop-gap job. I was just marking time while I was waiting for the great one to turn up. But this time, my uncle had someone else acting as his errand boy, so he didn't ask me to scrub any sinks.

I kept in touch with a local employment agency, and I stopped by often to read through the lists of new job openings. I got acquainted with the agency manager as the weeks rolled by, and one day after I'd been working for my uncle about four months, the employment agency itself had an opening for a job counselor. The pay would be better than what I was getting with my uncle, the future couldn't be any more nonexistent, and working in the agency, I'd have first crack at any good jobs that came along.

About this time, I moved out of my folks' house and into an apartment with Art Creedsman, one of my college buddies. My folks had been about to bug me to death. No matter what time of night I got in, mom would always call out and ask me where I'd been, with whom, what I'd been doing, whether I'd had a good time or not, and all that. I had to get out from under. After I moved to the apartment, mom still called me on the telephone a lot, but that wasn't quite so bad. If I didn't feel like talking, I could always tell her there was someone at the door and promise to call her back later.

One night there really *was* someone at the door. Art and I were sitting in the living room, drinking beer and just talking, when somebody pounded on the door, real heavy, like he wasn't going to stop until we let him in. Art and I looked at each other, wondering who it was, and he went to the door. I got up, too, to be the back-up man in case he needed one. When Art opened the door just a crack, it shot out of his hand and banged against the wall.

Chuck Hoffman literally threw himself into the room, and practically collapsed on the couch. I had known Chuck in college, and he'd always seemed a little bit nervous to me. Now he was huffing and puffing, completely out of breath, and he looked scared to death. Art got him a beer, and when he had simmered down a little, he started talking.

"It's the worst thing that's ever happened to me in my

whole entire life!" he gasped. "I don't know what I'm going to do with her."

He seemed so upset that I thought something awful must have happened. I had visions of his having killed someone and stuffed her into the truck of his car. Maybe he was worried about how he was going to dispose of the body, and whether or not the police would catch him. But it turned out that nothing quite that drastic was involved.

Chuck had been staying in a roominghouse. He had given his landlady a rather large deposit in advance. Too late, he had discovered that his landlady was an alcoholic, and her "house" was too rowdy for his taste. One night Chuck overheard her having a violent argument with her husband, an argument in which they were threatening to kill each other. Chuck was so paranoid, he thought they meant to kill him before they killed each other, and he was scared to go back to his room even to get his things, much less to ask for the return of his deposit.

I saw at once how to get his money back for him, and have someone to help Art and me with our apartment expenses at the same time. It was just the kind of action I relished, me with my persuasive manner.

"Relax, Chuck," I told him, winking at Art. "You can sleep on the couch here tonight, and tomorrow we'll help you get your green stuff back."

Art looked at me and shrugged, as if he didn't know what to do with either one of us. Chuck unlaced his shoes and stretched out on the couch.

The next morning, I put on my sunglasses and went with Chuck to the roominghouse, taking a little Brownie camera and a notebook along in my briefcase. When the landlady came to answer the door, I nodded toward Chuck and said, "I've come with Mr. Hoffman here to get his things and to get his deposit back. I understand he left quite a substantial amount of money with you?"

She hiccuped, put her hand to her mouth in apology, and started to close the door.

"Oh, we can't (hiccup) give deposits back," she said. "They're to (hiccup) cover the cost of (burp) . . ."

I had my foot in the doorway by then, and when the door came against it, I shoved it open and stepped authoritatively into the foyer, put my briefcase on a small table, and took out my camera.

While Chuck bounded up the stairs, taking them two at a time, to get his things, I lifted the camera to my eye. Aiming through the archway into a sitting room, I snapped the shutter, and advanced the imaginary film to position for the next shot. Then I aimed the camera right at the landlady.

She just stood there, her mouth hanging open, and finally sputtered, "What the—? Just (hiccup) what do you think (hiccup) you're doing?"

"Taking pictures for evidence for the lawsuit, ma'am," I said, matter of factly. After clicking off a few more frames, I put the camera back in the briefcase and picked up my notebook. Chuck was back downstairs, suits hanging over his arm, his suitcase bulging.

"Now, Mrs. Landon," I said, "I wonder if you'd mind answering a few questions for me. We understand you had a big argument with your husband, and—"

Before I could finish the first question, she had rushed into a back bedroom, come out with her pocketbook, and was peeling bills off and handing them to Chuck faster than I could count them.

I had a hard time maintaining my dignity until we were back outside and a block away in my car. Then I had to pull over to the curb just to explode in laughter.

"The way you pulled that off," Chuck said, real admiration in his eyes, "you've missed your calling, Sid. You should have been a con man."

I thought maybe he was right, but I didn't know quite how to get into that business. One thing was for sure: I was getting tired of the employment agency. All those forms to fill out. What a drag. There must be something better. It didn't occur to me then that Chuck was going to be my partner in finding it.

One night, Chuck and I were by ourselves in the apartment. I was sitting in the only really comfortable chair, reading the want ads, Chuck was sprawled on the floor, fiddling with a little transistor radio.

"Nothing but folk music," he muttered. "Guitars and folk music. Wouldn't you think there'd be a little more variety on the airwaves?" He sounded thoroughly disgusted, snapped the radio off, and sat up to lean against the record player. We started talking about fads in entertainment and decided that folk music must have reached an all-time high in popularity.

"You know," he said, "I'll bet there's a lot of high school talent in folk music these days."

"Yeah," I agreed. "Most any high school must have a dozen kids who can twang the guitar and sing some of that stuff."

The idea occurred to both of us at once, and we were off and running with it. Why not? A talent contest in every high school, the winners to be taped for radio presentation, listeners to write in their votes for their favorite.

In less than fifteen minutes, we had worked out the whole format for a show to be called "Hootenanny." The talent would work for little or nothing to be given a showcase. Chuck and I could share the work of setting the contests up, we could pocket the profits of outside concerts and clean up on donations contributed by the sponsors.

It was a natural, for both of us. Chuck's job was to line up the high schools, schedule the programs, and handle all the boring behind-the-scenes details. I would be the front man, the guy at the microphone who introduced the contestants, who auditioned the talent. Chuck did as much work as I did, maybe more, and we received equal billing on programs and advertisements as producers of "Hootenanny." But I was the one everyone saw.

The first radio station we approached with our idea was enthusiastic. They gave us a six-week contract, and hired us as producers at seventy-five dollars a week for each of us. Since that wasn't enough to live on, I hung on to my employment agency job for the time being.

For our first concert, we packed the gym at American University, and the radio station was ecstatic over the response to the program. The audience grew week by week, and when the first six weeks were almost over, the station was eager to renew the contract with Chuck and me as producers.

We wanted to continue with the program, all right, but I got to thinking that there wasn't really enough money in it for both of us. Instead of doing the decent thing, talking it over with Chuck, and offering to buy out his interest, I decided to make him quit.

Cutting out my co-producer wasn't hard. I began by deliberately disagreeing with him whenever an occasion arose. I started arguments over nothing. I would belittle him in front of other people, criticizing him for how he handled his share of the work, generally making life as miserable as I could for him. When he showed signs of weakening, I embarked on a little more intensive psychological warfare. Knowing he was easy to rattle, a nervous type to begin with, I hit upon the idea of tapping on the wall of his bedroom every night when he was trying to go to sleep. I got a kind of diabolical pleasure out of seeing him stagger out in the morning, frustrated from lack of sleep. He knew I was doing the tapping, but I would always act innocent, and try to make him think he was just hearing things, that he was probably going off his rocker.

"Chuck, for your own good, you ought to see a shrink," I told him.

One night when Art was out, Chuck came storming out of his room and into mine, all but frothing at the mouth, he was so angry with me.

"Okay, Mr. Producer!" he yelled. "You can have the show, you can have the apartment, you can have your infernal wall tapping! You can have whatever you want! I've had it!"

I don't know where he slept that night, but the next day, he came back, packed his things, and disappeared from my life. That left me as sole producer of my own show, getting all the glory *and* all the money for myself.

I quit my job with the employment agency and spent all my time in show biz, conducting talent contests, acting as an agent for our performers, scheduling nightclub acts, and taking as hefty a cut from all the proceeds as I could get by with. The dark glasses were full-time props for me now. I was Mr. Cool himself. The first million would soon be in sight.

I went away from Thee, my God, in my youth I strayed too far from Thy sustaining power, and I became to myself a barren land. . . . I stank in Thine eyes, yet was pleasing in my own and anxious to please the eyes of men.

Chapter 8

Blurred Signposts

"Sid, they always have the prettiest girls at these Young Democrats meetings," my buddy, Joe Garfinkle, was saying.

"You ought to know," I grinned at him. "And I'm willing to find out."

Joe was ten years older than I was, but I liked to go places with him because he always knew where the best parties were—and the best-looking women. I wasn't interested in *all* the girls, just some of them. They had to be good-looking, but they didn't have to be "good."

As we sauntered into the meeting room that night, I

saw a girl across the room with the most beautiful smile
I had ever seen.

"Hey, Joe!—Get a load of *that* one!" I made a silent
whistle, waiting for him to introduce me.

"You're on your own, kid," he chuckled. "I've never
seen that particular doll before. Can't help you none. Now
that one over there—" he gestured somewhere off to our
right—"she's more my style. I *do* know her already, from
way back. And how! Umm humh!"

He headed over in that direction, and I made a beeline
for the blonde with the smile that lit up the room. I gave
her my standard line.

"Say, I'm planning a great party at my apartment in a
week or two," I said. "How about writing your name and
phone number on this piece of paper so maybe I can let you
know—"

She turned off the smile and looked at me as if she
wasn't sure at first whether she ought to give me the information or not, but then she took my pencil and wrote
something on the paper. I stuffed it in my pocket, and we
talked about nothing for a few minutes. She told me she
should be studying for a Spanish test she was going to have
the next day. That didn't sound too exciting, so I left her
standing alone in order to collect a few more names and
phone numbers. Never could tell when a few extra girls
would come in handy for a party—or something.

Later in the evening, I noticed that Joe was talking to
the girl. That bothered me, somehow. I had never felt
exactly that way before, and wondered why I was feeling it
now. Something like jealousy maybe? After all, there was
no reason why Joe shouldn't talk to her. She wasn't my girl,
or anything like that. I didn't even know her, hadn't even
read the slip of paper she had put her name on. I dug it out

of my pocket and read the name. Joy, it said. Joy Young. It was a nice-sounding name.

A couple of weeks later, I telephoned Joy and asked her for a date. When I picked her up, I learned that she had a Corvette of her own. In my mind, any girl who had her own Corvette was bound to be rich.

When I was in college, I had made up my mind to marry a wealthy girl. After all, there was no point in investing my life in someone who didn't have something material of her own to contribute.

I was further impressed by the fact that when we went out to eat, Joy ordered the cheapest entree instead of the most expensive. And I was amazed at how easy she was to get along with. When I suggested that we might go to a movie, she agreed with me right away on which one we ought to see.

Before I had dated Joy half a dozen times, I was counting off her good qualities: she was clean-cut, agreeable, had class, was even-tempered, considerate, rich, and so pretty that I could feel myself falling in love with her. She had all the qualifications I looked for in a girl, except that she seemed to be a "nice" girl. That usually made a girl uninteresting to me, but even that was a decided plus in someone I might want to spend the rest of my life with.

There was only one hitch. Joy was a Gentile. But most of the Jewish girls I had dated had been too bossy to suit me, hard to get along with. Well, Joy would just have to convert to Judaism, that was all. Then everything about her would be super-kosher.

Joy had gotten serious about me, too. I realized it one night when she paused outside her apartment door and said that maybe we shouldn't see one another anymore.

"How come?" I asked her, so sure of what I wanted I

couldn't see any reason to break off.

"Well, we're getting too serious to be just friends, and we do have these different religions, after all."

The more she talked about the difficulties, the better I realized that she was the one for me. I didn't argue, I just took her in my arms and shushed her with kisses. The next day, I gave my class ring to Uncle Sol so he could make it into a charm for her bracelet. When she accepted it with that radiant smile of hers, that made it official in my mind. Joy was my girl, and someday she would be my wife.

"Mom, you know this Joy I've told you about, the Gentile girl I've been dating? I want to bring her to Shirley's wedding, and let her meet you and dad and some of the rest of the family."

I wasn't really too eager to put Joy in the midst of the mob of relatives, but she'd have to meet them sometime, and at my sister's wedding they would all be together.

"Sid, you're kidding me? You want to bring a shiksa to Shirley's wedding? She'll just feel out of place." Mom was about to dismiss my request lightly, but then she looked at me more closely, and suspicion dawned in her eyes.

"Sidney, you're not thinking— You *can't* be thinking of *marrying* a girl who's not Jewish?" Mom put one hand over her heart, sank down panting into an overstuffed chair, and began to fan herself with a newspaper. There flashed through my mind the one time in my childhood when mom didn't let me have my own way. She hadn't scolded me or punished me, she had just started screaming, like I did when I was having a tantrum. She had kept it up until I backed down. Surely she wasn't going to give me a hard time about Joy. I'd have to pull out all the stops to keep her from doing that.

"Mom, you want me to be happy, don't you?" I

pleaded, making my voice sound like a little boy again. "I'm in love with Joy. There's no other girl for me, and besides, she can hardly wait to convert to Judaism so she can fit in with the rest of the family."

That was a bald-faced lie. The only time we had seriously talked about our different religious backgrounds, Joy had suggested that I become a Baptist instead. That was out of the question, but I knew I could talk her into doing what I wanted her to do. There was no way my father would ever accept her otherwise. Besides, Joy's upbringing as a Baptist hadn't seemed that important to her. She hadn't once gone to church in all the time I'd known her.

"She wants to convert?" Mom was still eyeing me suspiciously, but the tempo of her fanning had slowed to a mere occasional flapping of the newspaper.

"Yeah," I said again. "We'll be going to see the rabbi to get her started on her instructions as soon as you break the news to dad and make the arrangements for us."

"Well, I don't know what your father will think about her coming to the wedding." I could see that mom's agile mind was in gear, figuring the best tactics to use to persuade dad, and then I laid down my high card.

"Mom, you'll just have to tell him that if Joy can't come with me, I won't be at the wedding either." From the stricken look that flashed across her face, I knew I had it made.

"It's ridiculous that anyone would think that Joy shouldn't come to the wedding," mom snorted, in full sail for the attack against my father. "After all, she's going to be our daughter-in-law, and Jack ought to be proud you'll be marrying someone who will convert and bring your children up right."

My cause was as good as accomplished. My secret

weapon had never failed me yet.

Shirley's wedding was a real extravaganza, far more elegant even than my bar mitzvah. There was an elaborate sit-down dinner for all the wedding guests, an eight-piece orchestra for the dancing afterward, gorgeous ice sculptures, flowers everywhere you looked, and food, food, food.

When I introduced Joy to my parents, my father scowled at her, said hello in the sternest voice he owned, and shook hands woodenly. Then mother concentrated on keeping dad on one side of the room while I kept Joy on the other.

All the other relatives crowded around to meet Joy, to look her over. They knew she must be something special t me or I wouldn't have brought her to the wedding. Although they were too polite to ask out loud, I could see the questions in everyone's eyes:

"What's with this Joy who's with Sidney?"

"Is he going to marry her?"

"She looks like a shiksa."

"What's her old man's business?"

But I wasn't ready to answer anybody's questions, spoken or unspoken. I didn't know my own timetable yet. I had just received a draft notice from Uncle Sam, and was to report for an induction examination the next week. I thought I'd be given a 4-F classification because of my bad hip, but I couldn't be sure. My classification would have some bearing on my plans for the immediate future. I would just have to wait and see, and so would all my relatives. I'd tell them my intentions when it was time for them to buy our wedding presents. That would be soon enough.

When I got on the bus with the rest of the fellows scheduled for induction examinations at Fort Hollabird

Maryland, I sat down next to a fellow I'd known since grade school. He told me that he had been married and divorced and that now he was "gay." Living with his male companion in New York City, where they were fashion designers, he was happy with his arrangement. *To each his own*, I thought. It was his business what he wanted to do with his life, just as it was my business what I did with mine.

At Fort Hollabird, all of us had to strip to the skin and walk single file through several lines in which doctors tapped and listened, probed and peered. Then we got dressed and went to the last inspection station. I handed x-rays of my hip to the attendants there, and was rewarded with an automatic 4-F classification. When my buddy handed over his psychiatrist's report, he was given an exempt-from-service classification, too.

As soon as I could, I got to a telephone to give Joy the news. I could tell from the tone of her voice that she was about to cry with relief.

"Oh, Sidney," she said, "I'm so happy! I could just see you being sent far away, to Germany, or someplace like that. And maybe I'd never see you again."

It shook me up that she cared that much.

The next morning, when I was combing my hair, I noticed that it was getting awfully thin on top. "I bet I'll really look ugly when I'm bald," I complained out loud to myself. Both of my grandfathers were bald; it ran in the family. Maybe I should get married while I was still handsome enough for Joy to be interested in me.

I was surprised when my rabbi tried to talk me out of marrying Joy. I thought he'd be happy that she had agreed to convert.

"Are you sure that Joy is the only girl in the whole world who can make you happy, Sidney?" he asked me, tamping tobacco down in his corncob pipe. Sitting there in his book-lined study, I could see that he didn't want a superficial answer. He wanted me to really probe my soul about the whole matter of marrying a Gentile. Feeling I had done my part by talking Joy into converting, I didn't think I should have to tackle the rabbi, so I suddenly remembered a previous nonexistent engagement and went home to sic my invincible secret weapon on him.

Mom dived in with no holds barred, certain that she would lose her son if his wife-to-be was not permitted to become a Jew. No man in his right mind dared stand up to my mother, rabbi or not. The next thing I knew, the rabbi was on the telephone, wanting to speak to me. He sounded eager to start Joy's instruction in Judaism.

Under the hammering of my mom's daily influence, even my dad was becoming almost persuaded that a converted Jewish daughter-in-law was actually preferable to one who had merely been born into the faith.

We decided on a small wedding at my parents' home. Since Joy had converted to Judaism, her parents weren't interested in throwing a big wedding, and a lavish Jewish wedding didn't seem appropriate either.

On March 15, 1964, Joy and I said our vows before the rabbi under a huppah, a special wedding canopy held up with poles, in my parents' living room. There were only a few relatives present as Joy and I drank from the fragile wine glass and then I smashed it with my foot, symbolizing the destruction of the Temple in Jerusalem. That was supposed to remind us that our marriage might be broken, too, unless it was under God's protection.

But if I knew nothing about the significance of the destruction of the Temple, I knew less about the need for God's protection in a marriage. The only thing I thought about as I heard the crunch of the glass under my foot was that now I had a beautiful wife, to do for me all the things a wife was expected to do.

"My people are destroyed for lack of knowledge," God's word said (Hosea 4:6). But I was traveling so fast down the road leading to destruction that the signposts blurred beyond reading as I sped by them.

I foamed in my wickedness, following the rushing of my own tide, leaving You and going beyond all Your laws. Nor did I escape Your scourges. No mortal can. You were always by me, mercifully hard upon me, and besprinkling all my illicit pleasures with certain elements of bitterness, to draw me on to seek for pleasures in which no bitterness should be. And where was I to find such pleasures save in You, O Lord, You who use sorrow to teach, and wound us to heal, and kill us lest we die to You.

Chapter 9

Something More?

A few weeks before our wedding, I talked to the manager of the radio station over which "Hootenanny" was aired.

"Say," I told him, "I'm going to get married soon. How about using your influence with one of our sponsors—to see if he'd give me the honeymoon suite in the Summit Hotel for a few days?"

"Congratulations, Sid," he said, shifting his cigar to the corner of his mouth, and giving me a hearty handshake. "I expect it's all booked up. But best regards, anyway."

"Best regards, anyway." That's what I got from several people who called to cancel bookings for folk music programs. A longhaired singing group from England called "The Beatles" had come onto the scene. Folk music was passe overnight, and a week before the wedding, my show went off the air.

New wife, new apartment, new furniture, and no job. Joy's knight in shining armor, the big wheel, strong, successful, and glamorous, turned into an unshaven reader of want ads, lazing around the apartment in wrinkled Bermuda shorts, waiting for his working wife to come home and cook dinner for him. Without the prestige of my position to keep my ego boosted, I reverted to being a complaining, surly, selfish, demanding mamma's boy. I began to see something other than hero worship in Joy's eyes when she came in tired from work at five-thirty every day and found that I, who had been loafing around all day watching TV, expected her to wait on me.

For a couple of months, I made a halfhearted attempt to sell real estate on a commission basis, but I wasn't successful at it, and brought in very little income. Then one day when I was sitting around, I picked up a *Reader's Digest* and read an article written by a health officer in the venereal disease branch of HEW. The account of his adventures in going to houses of ill repute, talking to prostitutes, and interviewing nightclub habitues about their sexual contacts sounded most intriguing to me. Why, he was like an F.B.I. agent almost.

I called the local office of HEW to see if there were any job openings available in that type of work, told them something of my education and job experience, and was scheduled to be interviewed for an opening in Miami, Florida. I learned later that the interviewer thought I had a greater potential for success in the job than anyone else who had ever applied with them. The job was mine.

Joy was excited at the prospect of moving to Florida. It seemed that it would be like a perpetual vacation, and she hated her secretarial job in Washington. We packed up to move, and I enrolled in the training course to be a health officer in the VD department of HEW.

The training course emphasized the symptoms and history of VD, the best interviewing techniques, and how to get an individual to open up and tell you who his sex partners had been. I learned not to be shocked or surprised at anything.

After a few weeks training, I put on my dark glasses again and was back in the glamor (I thought) of the working world. But the men conducting the training course had neglected to mention my bugaboo. I was required to draw blood from suspects.

My first experience at performing that operation nearly threw me. I kept thinking there would be someone else who would handle that aspect of it, but I was mistaken. *I* had to roll the man's sleeve up; *I* had to knot the rubber hose around his arm; *I* had to ask him to make a fist while I punched around, looking for a large-enough vein; *I* had to jab and jab again trying to get the needle in the right place; *I* had to pull the plunger back and back until the vial was filled with the dark red venous blood. Then *I* had to remember to tell him to relax his fist before I withdrew the needle, so that the blood wouldn't spurt out all over me. Every single step of the operation was calculated to make me sick at my stomach.

On top of all that, some of the places I was required to go were about as far from glamorous as anyone could possibly imagine. My interviewees were never scantily clad, perfumed beauties backstage in glittering nightclubs. I remember one day, sweltering in the heat, perching on the

edge of a broken-down, absolutely filthy couch, breathing
dirt and dust, trying to get a blood sample from a toothless
hag who had on a rag of a housedress with nothing under it.
The stench was overpowering, her list of contacts seem-
ingly endless. I could hear mice scurrying through the
walls, and dead cockroaches were lying all over the floor.

If I hadn't been flat broke, with no savings to fall back
on, no way to get to Washington, no other way to pay rent
or buy groceries, I'd have quit after the first unglamorous,
bloody day. But I had no choice but to stay with it.

Eventually, the endless repetition dulled the horror of
it for me, and I took so many blood samples that it became
routine. But I always hated the job.

The job didn't like me, either. My boss was a perfec-
tionist, and it didn't seem to cut any ice at all with him that
I was such an excellent interviewer, such a bright young
man with so many ideas for improving operations and cutting down on paperwork in the office. At my first sugges-
tion, he let it be known that *after* I had worked for a year,
then I'd be entitled to be heard, and not until.

I filled out the endless forms in the most slipshod way,
feeling the whole business of detailed record-keeping far
beneath my dignity. But my dignity fell flat on its face the
day the boss tacked a number of *my* forms on the bulletin
board, with the multitudinous mistakes circled in bright
red pencil. I was held up as a first-class bad example of a
sloppy workman. After that, I didn't care if he ever im-
plemented any of my good ideas or not. All I wanted was
out. Surely there was another job somewhere that was big
enough for my superlative abilities.

One of my friends had told me about Henry Green-
berg, but I couldn't believe what I heard. The story was
that Henry was just thirty-one years old and that he had al-

ready made a million dollars selling life insurance. To me, being a life insurance salesman had always seemed about the lowest occupation on the totem pole, just half a step above being a used-car salesman. I wasn't remotely interested in being either one. Still, a million dollars—

I was almost twenty-five already, and had hardly two nickels to rub together every month after the bills were paid, even though Joy and I were both working. So when Henry, whom I had never met, called me one night from his phone in his brand-new Lincoln Continental and invited me to dinner at the swankiest restaurant in Miami, I jumped at the chance.

Henry's appearance appalled me. He was short, and had an adolescent-lumpy complexion. In spite of his obviously expensive clothes, he didn't look like a millionaire. But the roll of bills in his pocket could have choked a horse. His wife, on the other hand, looked like she had stepped out of *Vogue,* and his house was a genuine mansion, overpowering even *my* imagination.

I hadn't listened to Henry for five minutes before I knew he was the most fantastic salesman I had ever heard. By the time we had finished dinner, I was sold on selling life insurance. I forgot the jokes about men in that profession. Henry had persuaded me that a Lincoln Continental, a $100,000 house, and anything else I wanted that money could buy, were right around the corner for me if I would follow his instructions exactly.

The next day, I turned in my blood-testing equipment to the Miami Health Department, bequeathed to them my mountain of incomplete forms, and took a deep breath. Then I picked up the eight-minute sales presentation Henry had told me to memorize. I had tried to talk him out of requiring me to do that because memorizing was always difficult for me, and besides, I thought I could write a better presentation of my own. He was insistent that I do things his way, however, and there was a million-dollar incentive for me to follow in his footsteps.

"I have an unusual idea that many men in your . . ." I drilled the presentation over and over until I could say it in my sleep.

The presentation learned, I went out to interview my first prospect. He bought a policy from me.

I interviewed the second prospect. He bought a policy from me.

I interviewed the third prospect. He bought a policy from me.

The presentation had proved its worth. I didn't think any longer about writing up one of my own. Day after day, I approached my prospects with the infallible canned speech, "Sir, I have an unusual idea that many men in your circumstances . . ." and day after day they signed on the dotted line. By the second month, I was the leading salesman in the Miami office of the John Hancock Insurance Company, and I was winning every contest in sight. In my first six months, I sold over $500,000 worth of life insurance in a city where I knew practically nobody on the right side of the tracks.

One day the manager called me into his office and told me that the police department had called and asked if a Sid Roth was in their employ. Then the manager asked me if I had been on North West Fortieth Street at ten o'clock the night before, knocking on doors.

"Yes," I admitted, my heart beating fast, wondering what was wrong with that.

"Well, Sid, somebody saw you and thought you must be a burglar. Life insurance salesmen don't usually go knocking on doors that late at night unless they have an appointment ahead of time."

I blushed, stammered some kind of lame-brained explanation about how I didn't realize it was so late at the time, and waited for the dressing-down that never came.

"You've got chutzpah, Sid, real chutzpah," he chuckled, genuine admiration in his voice.

Compliments always went to my head and made me more overbearing than ever. Later that day, I was chewing out a secretary who hadn't been filing my insurance applications properly. I was really giving her a hard time, my humiliating complaints about her inefficiency echoing loudly down the hall. The manager happened to hear the whole ugly bit, and called me into his office for a word of advice.

"Take it from me, Sid," he said. "You can catch more flies with honey than with vinegar."

So who wants to catch flies? I thought. I just grunted an uh huh, smiled and went back to my office. I was embarrassed that he had overheard me being so rude. Since he had just complimented me about my chutzpah, I didn't want him to see me in a bad light. I resolved to keep my voice low the next time I criticized those dumb office girls.

For the first time in my post-college career, I was making real money in a job that had an exciting future for me. But I was bored, bored almost to death, with my job, our marriage, everything.

I was a success, going nowhere, like a phonograph needle just following the grooves around. But one day I would come to the end of the grooves. And then what? An explosion followed by nothingness? It hardly seemed worthwhile to hang around for a denouement as meaningless as that.

There must be something more. But what was it?
Where was it?

Your law, O Lord, punishes theft; and this law is so written in the hearts of men that not even the breaking of it blots it out: for no thief bears calmly being stolen from – not even if he is rich and the other steals through want. Yet I chose to steal, and not because want drove me to it – unless a want of justice and contempt for it and an excess for iniquity.

Chapter 10

Thief

Whatever and wherever the something more was, it didn't seem to be in Miami. Joy was as fed up with her job there as I was with mine, and we were about fed up with each other, snarling at one another, quarrelling about everything. Life seemed to have no future; it was empty, colorless, devoid of meaning and excitement. Maybe a change of scenery would help. We took a two-weeks' vacation and headed for Washington, D.C.

The grass did look greener there, especially after the Washington branch of the Hancock Insurance Company agreed to pay all our relocation expenses if I would sell for them in D.C. The offer had everything going for it. In

Miami, many of my first sales were requiring callbacks. Clients were not paying their premiums, and I was required to find out why, to resell them if necessary. I despised callbacks. If I left the Miami area, the local manager would have to take care of callbacks for me.

In addition to that, the financial future for me would surely be more promising in Washington where I knew so many people. After all, if I could sell $500,000 worth of insurance as a greenhorn in Miami, a city where I knew practically no one on the right side of the tracks, I should really be able to clean up in Washington where I had lived most of my life. And maybe Joy would be happier there, too, being able to see her parents more often. The beautiful smile that had attracted me to her in the first place had been buried under a grim hanging-on-for-dear-life look for some time now.

The only way we could ever leave Miami any time soon was to have someone foot the bill for us. I had just drained our savings account to invest in a sure-fire scheme that was taking a little longer to pay off than I had anticipated.

Another insurance salesman, my good friend, Mike Behrman, had told me about the deal where I could turn our $2,000 of savings into a cool coin collection worth at least $15,000, if I had the nerve to fork over the money and wait it out for a couple of weeks. The day I went home to get the passbook so I could withdraw the money from our savings account, Joy had given me a hard time about it.

"Sid!" she said, in her most disgusted tone when I told her what I was going to do. "Nobody in his right mind would give you a collection worth $15,000 for only $2,000. You *know* that."

I argued her out of it somehow, even though I knew

that most of our savings were the result of her slaving away at a job she couldn't stand. Persuading myself that I knew best, and telling her that she'd rejoice with me when we had more money than ever, I took the passbook and emptied the account.

I gave Mike the money, in crisp new twenties, just the way he'd asked for it, got a written receipt, and his promise that he'd turn the money over to his contacts, the guys who would soon have the coins in their possession. He wasn't too explicit about exactly who *they* were, and I thought it best not to be too inquisitive. His innuendos led me to believe they were in close cahoots with the Mafia if not actually members of it themselves.

For a few weeks, I had waited patiently, without any anxiety at all, dreaming how I would spend the money after I got my hands on the coin collection and sold it for its true value. I knew, of course, that the deal wasn't strictly on the up and up, that maybe the coins were stolen property, but I couldn't afford to be too fussy about that. For a 750% profit in a few weeks' time, I expected to take *some* risk.

While I waited, Joy didn't give me any peace about it, needling me every day about when my friend was going to deliver the valuable merchandise. I gritted my teeth and said less and less about it as the weeks went by. I saw my friend every day at work, and he kept assuring me that the details were being worked out, that I shouldn't blow my cool. He made me feel appreciative that he was taking such big risks for me in his dealing with the syndicate.

One afternoon, Mike told me he had something important and confidential to discuss, so we arranged to meet at a bar after work that day. In my excited optimism, I thought he was probably going to make the pickup and delivery that day. I couldn't keep my mind on my prospects, I

was so expectant. But when he walked into the bar, he
didn't have anything in his hands.

"It's like this, Sid," Mike said when we had seated
ourselves at a little round table in a dim corner and the
waitress had brought us our drinks. "You've paid your
money in good faith, the guys *mean* to keep their end of the
bargain, but—"

He paused to lift his glass and drain it, and my heart
slid into my shoes.

"But what?" I demanded. "There can't be any buts
about it. A deal's a deal." I was amazed at how cold and
hard, criminal almost, my own voice sounded.

"Now don't get uptight, Sid," Mike said, furrowing his
brow and lifting his hand to stop my impatience. "There's
still a way to pull the fat out of the fire. It's just going to take
a little more money."

"How much?"

"Well, I'm not at liberty to divulge details, you
understand—"

"Cut the explaining! Just tell me how much!" I could
feel my hands tightening on my glass.

"Six hundred."

"*Six hundred!*" My whole being was outraged. "*Six
hundred!*"

"Yep. Six hundred. Today. The whole shebang is
down the drain unless you can come up with six hundred
more. Today."

He might as well have said six thousand. I'd given him
all our savings already. There wasn't another dime—But
wait. There *was* one possibility. No, it was better than a
possibility, it was a sure thing. I slapped the table.

"Let me make a phone call. It'll take just a sec."

I almost tipped the little table over in my haste to get

to a phone. I dialed the number so familiar to me, and felt a surge of relief when mom answered.

"Can't explain it now, mom, but I've got to have $600 right away, today."

I heard the swift intake of her breath and could imagine the stricken look on her face as she almost wailed, "Oh, Sidney, you're not hurt, are you? Or in trouble? Nothing's wrong with my boy—"

"No, no mom. It's just that I *have* to have six hundred right now. Look, I'll explain everything when we get to Washington next week. You'll get the money back, every penny of it, I promise. But wire it to me right now, okay?" I was almost snapping at her, right in the midst of asking such a huge favor. She had every right to turn me down, but she never had before. I waited. And then it came.

"Sure, Sidney. You want me to wire $600. I'll do it right away."

I forced a "Thanks, mom," from my lips and hung up the phone, imagining her end of the conversation as I worked my way through the after-work crowd and back to our table. She'd be saying, "Now take care of yourself, Sidney," and then, even after she realized I'd hung up, she'd say the inevitable, "Goodbye and good luck." She'd said that to me as long as I could remember, whenever we'd parted. "Goodbye and good luck." I knew that she might be saying goodbye to her money that day without knowing it, but with luck, Mike would still be waiting for me.

Mike was waiting. For the first time, I noticed that he looked nervous, too. And I thought about the spot he was in. Oh well, he was probably getting a hefty cut for being the go-between. I'd let him worry about his end of it.

"It's okay, Mike. Everything's going to be all right," I found myself assuring him. "The six hundred is already on its way. Mom's wiring it."

"Your mom? Sending you *that* kind of money? Just like that? What'd you tell her?"

"Why, I didn't tell her anything." I didn't think anything of it, but Mike was so impressed, he seemed to forget his own worries for a moment.

"I never had a mother who would do something like that for me," he mused. And then he stared at me so intently it made me uneasy. "Do you have any idea how lucky you are, Sid? Just to ask her and she'll send it, just like that? Fantastic!" He shook his head, as if he still couldn't believe it.

"Nothing fantastic about it," I shrugged. "That's just my mom, that's all. That's how she is. She's always been that way. She'd do anything for me, even lay down her life for me if I asked her to."

The six hundred came, I gave it to Mike, and he assured me everything would be rolling smoothly from there on out. I should have the coins in my possession in a few days' time.

The day before we were expecting the movers to arrive to pack our things for Washington, Mike told me he was sorry that there had been another unforeseen hitch. I breathed easier when I learned this one wouldn't cost me anything, just a little more waiting. I wouldn't have the coins before I moved to Washington, but as soon as he could, he would personally fly the collection to me.

When I went home that day, Joy, who had already resigned from her job, was sitting in a lawn chair behind our apartment, reading a magazine. When I broke the news to her, her face registered utter contempt and disgust. She flung her magazine down on the grass and started screaming at me—

"Sid!" she yelled, "You'll *never* have those coins, and you know it! How could you do this to me, take all the money I worked so hard for, and just throw it away like that? Any fool would know better."

People slammed open their apartment windows and stuck their heads out to see what was going on. I was afraid to look up, because I knew everybody was watching and listening to the tirade, but Joy didn't seem to care. The harder I tried to shush her, the louder she ranted.

Finally, I just turned and went back into the apartment and let her scream at the empty air. But it got to me, just the same. When she came in, she was sobbing, and I reached out to her.

"Joy, I—"

But she wouldn't listen. She stumbled into the bedroom and slammed the door.

The day after we arrived in Washington, I sent a threatening telegram to Mike, telling him I was going straight to the police if I didn't have the merchandise by the following Friday. He telephoned, tried to calm me down, told me the coins were already in his hands for me, and that I should meet him at the airport two weeks from that Friday at gate 29 at 2:04 P.M. Delivery was having to be delayed that long, he said, in order to protect me, because the feds had gotten wind of some kind of operation, and Mike and his contacts were being watched around the clock.

I was temporarily mollified, but Joy continued full of cold outrage at how I had thrown away money she felt belonged to her. Oh, well, she would sing a different tune when the profits were in my hands.

The time passed. I got to the airport half an hour early on the appointed afternoon, and seated myself in the waiting area near the gate where Mike's flight would come in. When his flight number was called, I took a firm grip on the large empty attache case I had brought to hold the coins, and stood alongside the passageway where arrivals were beginning to stream through, searching their faces for Mike. As the unfamiliar faces passed by, I kept giving myself excuses for why he wasn't the first one off the plane, and I felt pretty good, for a while.

"He probably got stuck clear at the back of the coach," I reasoned. "Most likely, he'll be the last one off." And when the last passenger had trickled through, I just figured he had missed his flight. Nothing to get excited about. Mike had never been a stickler for promptness, and he'd probably arrived at the airport too late to make it. That being the case, he'd be along on the next flight. It was due in a couple of hours, so I bought a magazine, went up to the coffeeshop and got one to go, and brought it back down to the waiting area so I wouldn't miss him when he did come.

I finished the coffee, smoked a couple of cigarettes, leafed through the pages of the magazine without seeing them, looked at my watch a blue billion times, raising it to my ear to see if it was still running, and decided I should take it to my Uncle Sol for repair the next day. No watch in good order could possibly run that slow. When the arrival of the Miami flight was announced, I about jumped out of my skin. The deplaning passengers came through, the flight was reboarded, cleared for takeoff, and still no Mike.

Maybe he was sick or something and hadn't been able to make the flight . . . Maybe he had called to let me know, but the message hadn't reached me . . . Yes, that was surely it. I dialed Joy's parents' apartment where we were staying at the time, and when Joy's mother answered, I asked if there had been a message for me.

"Why, no, Sidney," she said, probably knowing why I was calling. "Nobody has called all day."

"Maybe your phone is out of order?" I blurted, and then blushed with the foolishness of my question. After all, *my* call had gotten through all right. I hung up then, almost numb with disappointment, and tried one more call.

"Mike Behrman, operator, B-e-h-r-m-a-n, in Miami, Florida." There was the usual agony of getting the operator to understand the name, getting her to understand that I didn't have his number, having to verify his address, and then the mechanical, "I'm sorry, but the number you have called is no longer in service."

I called the Miami Hancock Agency next, to see if they could tell me how to get in touch with Mike. The secretary broke it to me with crisp efficiency.

"I'm sorry, Mr. Roth. We can't help you. Mr. Behrman left us suddenly, without any explanation. No, there is no forwarding address."

I dragged out of the airport, across the street to the parking area, found my car, and drove woodenly through the traffic back to the apartment, parked, went up in the elevator, and let myself in.

"He didn't show, huh." It wasn't a question the way Joy said it. It was a defeated I-told-you-so. I almost wished she'd yell at me, give me something to fight back against, to get me out of the awful numbness of the realization that I'd been conned, completely conned. I was just like some stupid idiot who thought he had really bought the Brooklyn Bridge for fifty bucks and had stood all night on the corner in the rain waiting for the guy to come back and hand him the title to it.

I propose now to set down my past wickedness and the carnal corruptions of my soul, not for love of them but that I may love Thee, O my God. I do it for love of Thy love, passing again in the bitterness of remembrance over my most evil ways that Thou mayest thereby grow ever lovelier to me. . . . And I collect my self out of that broken state in which my very being was torn asunder because I was turned away from Thee, the One, and wasted upon the many.

Chapter 11

The Fortune-Teller

The two thousand was gone, and the six hundred after it. But I was on my way to make a million, and $2,600 was less than a drop in the bucket. Joy quit bugging me about it, feeling that I had suffered enough, I guess, and mom kept building me up by talking about what an awful cruel man my ex-friend had been to bilk me of our savings in that way.

My own indignation was used up, my wounds began to heal, and my eternal optimism took over. I poured myself back into the role of becoming a millionaire in a hurry by selling life insurance.

During our first six months in Washington, I repeated

my Miami success pattern, and wound up my first year in life insurance with policies worth almost a million dollars in force. I was doing so well that Joy quit her hated secretarial job and went back to school fulltime to learn to be an interior designer. We had moved into our own apartment, a great relief to both of us after having been cooped up with Joy's parents for two months. We almost felt we were happy together again. But it wasn't real, and it didn't last. Soon we were back in our respective roles of merely tolerating one another's presence.

One day my Uncle Sol called, all excited about a new kind of life insurance policy that was tied in with a mutual fund. It sounded different, all right, but lousy. I told him so, and insisted that what I was selling was far superior to what anyone else had to offer. I knew that Uncle Sol had my best interests at heart, however, and I agreed to meet with him and the other agent and hear about the other guy's "superior" product.

Much to my surprise, after two hours, I agreed that his product was better than mine, and I was ready to change jobs. When I told my boss I was quitting, he was furious because not only was I quitting, but I was taking two of the best salesmen on his force with me into the new thing.

"Sid, you can't do that!" he roared. "It's against every rule of ethics! We paid to move you up here, and we've got a big investment in you and those other salesmen. We're entitled to a return on our investment!" The louder he shouted, the more right he was, the more immovable I became.

"Look," I told him, a menacing tone in my voice, "I've already contributed more than enough to this outfit. I'd be a fool not to put my own best interests first, and that goes for these other guys, too. You don't own us, you know."

After the sneering way I talked to him, it's a wonder he didn't throw me out.

During my second year in the insurance business, this time with Chatfield Associates, I sold over a million dollars worth of insurance again. By the end of the year, I was a manager with ten men under me. My sales unit was one of the top production units in the country, and hardly a week passed without a telegram congratulating me for some new sales achievement.

Somewhere along the line, after about a year and a half with Chatfield, it occurred to me that if I could sell so well for other people, I was a fool to line *their* pockets. I ought to move out on my own, start my own company, and then I'd really be bringing it in.

But my own company died aborning. Something seemed to go wrong with my selling ability, and I wasn't able to communicate it to the men I hired to work for me. The office moved too slowly, and after less than six months, I closed up shop and took a new position with another outfit. For part of a year, I worked for them as a regional manager, traveling a lot, setting up offices, and training personnel. But it went sour, too. I recognized that I was going nowhere fast, and I began looking for another position, one where they would really appreciate me. In spite of my initial success in selling life insurance, all I wanted was out.

In the midst of my job-hopping, Joy told me that we were expecting a baby. Well!

After our daughter was born, even *I* could see that hopping from one poorly done job to another was no way to raise a family. When I was given a chance to go to work as an executive with Merrill, Lynch, Pierce, Fenner & Smith, one of the finest investment companies in America, I rec-

ognized it as being exactly what I needed. No more ped-
dling life insurance. Any clod could do that. This was the
career spot I should have been in years ago. The sky was
the limit.

After three months local training, I went to New York
for more intensive instruction. During the two months I
spent there, away from Joy and our baby girl, I made the
rounds of the singles bars at night. I turned into a real
swinger. Whatever shreds of our marriage had been left
hanging together disintegrated completely.

Not because I wanted to, but out of a peculiar obedi-
ence to some kind of "ought to," I telephoned Joy from a
bar on New Year's Eve. She was crying when she answered
the phone, but she managed to sob out that her father, who
had been an alcoholic for years, had just shot himself in the
head.

Joy sounded so pitiful, so alone, so upset, that I got a
cab to the airport and was on the next plane for
Washington. But where I had been, and what I had become, were so sickeningly obvious to Joy when she saw me,
that she told me I needn't have bothered to come home.
Our marriage was finished.

Joy had had all the unfaithfulness, all the neglect, sne
could take from me. She wanted just one thing more. A
separation.

Separation. Unthinkable for a Jewish family. When I
was a child, my parents had talked seriously of separation
once. My father had said that he and I would move to New
York, and Shirley would stay in Washington with mom. He
promised that I'd love it in New York with him, but I
couldn't imagine life without mom fighting my battles for
me, and I couldn't imagine dad living without her, either,
no matter how violently they disagreed about some things.

Somehow, they had worked out their differences, or figured how to live with them, and the split hadn't come.

As I examined my own feelings, I admitted that a part of me wanted to leave Joy, all right, but there was another part that seemed to want us to stay together in spite of everything. It was going to be a difficult decision for me to make.

For the last two years, I had been turning to a fortune-teller for help with the major decisions in my life. I would ask him what I should do.

For as long as I could remember, I had been interested in everything to do with the occult. Astrology, fortune-telling, handwriting analysis, reincarnation, hypnosis, communicating with the dead, spiritualism, Ouija boards, psychic powers. All held a fascination for me that was far beyond a mere hobby or fad or interest. It was as if a supernatural force drew me, and when one of my mother's friends had told her one day about the new fortune-teller she'd discovered, and how positively fantastic he was, I was quick to get his address.

When I first went into the nondescript office building where he had his place of business, I found the fortune-teller himself to be a very solid ruddy-faced individual instead of the wraith the atmosphere of the place suggested. He was sitting behind a screen in the corner of a shabby room that served also as a waiting area for his clients, and I seated myself across the rickety card table from him. The first thing he told me, as he shuffled through his cards and fanned them out, sent chills down my spine.

"Sir, your parents live near Sixteenth Street in upper Northwest near Kennedy Street," he said, matter-of-factly.

Wow! How could he have known that? They lived just one block from Kennedy! That was near, all right. And

there was no way he could have known that just from looking at me.

I was so impressed with the fortune-teller's supernatural knowledge that I consulted him about every major
decision from then on. Several times, Joy and I quarreled
over the fact that I couldn't seem to decide anything without consulting him first. There were periods when I visited
him several times a week.

Once it occurred to me to wonder, since he had such
supernatural powers, why he wasn't a millionaire in the
stock market, why he didn't have a plusher office, why he
needed my miserable three dollars a visit. But I quickly
brushed such questioning aside. I was hooked.

When I asked the fortune-teller whether or not I
should leave Joy, he gave me a strong go-ahead, and I was
relieved that I didn't have to make the decision for myself.

Looking in the newspaper for a place to stay, I found
a roommate referral service which put me in touch with a
swinging bachelor named Jeff. His apartment was nicely
furnished, immaculately clean. There was only one catch.
Jeff's girl friend shared his bedroom.

"Sid, do you mind if my girl friend sleeps with me?" he
asked.

"Yes," I answered. "I do mind—because she isn't
sleeping with me." We laughed, and I had passed the test.

When Joy was at work the next day, I moved my
clothes out of our apartment and drove off into my new, exciting, glamorous, bachelor-at-large life. Wanting to make a
clean break with everything in my past, I asked the
fortune-teller if it would be all right for me to change jobs
again. He had always approved my job changes before,
even triggered my looking for a new job sometimes by telling me that I would be changing jobs soon, but this time he

turned thumbs down, advising me against leaving Merrill Lynch. He had an elderly client who sold stocks from time to time and gave the money to him. I was a convenient broker to handle these transactions without asking foolish questions.

Still, I knew I wasn't measuring up at Merrill, Lynch, and it would be easier to start over somewhere else than to dig in and do a good job there. I didn't take the fortune-teller's advice, but jumped when a new company offered me a stock option for going with them.

Having failed to take the fortune-teller's advice, I decided not to see him again, but I felt absolutely lost without someone to turn to for guidance.

I fell in with a sect of men talking high-sounding non-sense, carnal and wordy men. The snares of the devil were in their mouths, to trap souls . . .

Chapter 12

Power Hook-Up

One day, Mike Wasserman, my assistant sales manager at Glenwood Equities, was talking to me about one of his cases. He knew I had consulted a fortune-teller in the past, and he started telling me about a friend of his who once had no fortune-telling ability of his own at all, but who had taken a mind-control course that had revolutionized his life. Now he had supernatural abilities far beyond those of any ordinary fortune-teller. He knew things about other people that he had no natural way of knowing; he knew what was going to happen in the future; he knew everything he needed to know.

Wow! That sounded like exactly what I needed. I could no longer hide the fact that my ability in business was getting shaky. My sales had no staying power, and I was losing clients right and left. My best salesmen were leaving me. All in all, I had hit a real string of bad luck. If I had some of the psychic ability Mike's friend had received from the mind-control course, maybe then I could stay on top of things. Why, with that kind of ability, I probably wouldn't even need a job!

On my next Saturday off, I drove up to New Jersey to meet Mike's friend, to give him an acid test.

"Russ," I said, getting right to the point of my visit, "your friend Mike has been telling me that the mind-control course you took enables you to tap into supernatural power so you *know* things you have no natural way of knowing. Is that right?"

"Try me," he challenged. "See for yourself. Just give me the name of someone who's had something wrong with him, and I will tell you what it is. Anyone at all."

"Gilmore Young," I said, giving him the name of Joy's father.

Russ closed his eyes, seemed to be concentrating intently, his eyelids fluttering, and said, "I see a light starting toward this man—toward his head. It's entering his head—and starting to shatter—"

Russ's eyes popped wide with wonder as he stammered, "Could this man have been shot in his head—with a bullet?"

That was all I needed to know. Russ had supernatural power all right. Just think what I could do when that power was mine!

A new mind-control class would begin in the D.C. area in a month. I marked it on my calendar, crossing off the days as it came closer and closer. I knew it would be what I had been searching for all my life, a can't-fail approach to acclaim and financial success.

If I could have known that what lay ahead was not acclaim and success, but stark terror, I'd have run screaming in the opposite direction. But I didn't know. And I would not know until after I had plunged headlong into hell.

The day finally arrived, the day when supernatural powers beyond anything I had ever observed in the fortune-teller would begin to be mine. I drove with mounting excitement to the Sheraton, where the introductory mind-control lecture would be held.

The instructor appeared to be in his middle twenties, intelligent-looking, neatly dressed. There was nothing outward to distinguish him or his twenty-odd listeners from people at a typical organization meeting. He told us that after the one-week course, we would be able to, among other things, control our weight, improve our memories, know what other people were thinking, cure illnesses, and better our finances.

It sounded too good to be true. But it had to be legitimate. There was a money-back guarantee. Anyone who couldn't demonstrate real psychic ability by passing an acid test at the end of a week would have his money refunded.

As the instructor talked on, I knew I was going to make it big. All my former failures, those I had pretended were successes, faded. It was as if my life was beginning all over again. Right, this time. Goodbye frustration and failure, spinning my wheels, going nowhere. Hello happiness, going *somewhere*.

The first two days of class, we learned how to relax.

The object was to lower the speed of our brain waves to the state that occurs in sleep. After reaching this level, we were told to imagine that we had a counselor in our head. The counselor would be able to answer any questions we might ask, to perform any test we asked of him.

I listened intently to all the instructor told us, practiced relaxing to lower my brain waves, got acquainted with my counselor, and was ready for the acid test the last day of the course.

The instructor gave me the name of a woman I had never heard of. I closed my eyes, lowered my brain waves, and began to meditate. In a few moments, I saw a stick figure of a woman in my imagination. She had a large "x" over one of her breasts.

"Could she have cancer of the breast?" I blurted.

"That's right, Sid! That's right!" The instructor applauded, and the class joined him. I had passed the acid test. Supernatural power was mine.

When I went to the office the next morning, I could hardly wait to experiment with my new talent. My boss passed by my office, and I called him in, asking him to give me the name of someone I didn't know—someone who was sick. My boss looked at me as if he thought I had flipped my lid, but he gave me the name of a man.

I closed my eyes, lowered my brain waves, and suddenly, without warning, I felt my arms begin to shake.

"Why, that's exactly what my father does!" my boss exclaimed, obviously as surprised as I was.

"Could he have Parkinson's disease?" I heard myself saying. I didn't know what the disease was, nor anything about its symptoms. The name just came to me.

"Yes, that's it!" my boss said, excitedly rising from his chair.

Then I told him that I didn't need to shake my arms anymore.

"That's right!" he exclaimed again. "Yesterday my father started taking a new medication, and his shaking was controlled!"

Wow! This new ability was terrific. The power seemed to be increasing all the time. Yesterday I only had visions, today I feel the symptoms. I wonder what new will happen tomorrow?

The power was real, all right. And the more I experimented, the more uses I found for it.

One afternoon, I was lost in the maze of roads winding through a park, and I said, "Counselor, direct me home." I made turns without hesitation on streets that were totally unfamiliar to me, and found myself home in record time.

If I needed a parking space, all I had to do was ask that a space be available.

It didn't matter how hard the situation was, my counselor was able to take care of it. He was even more powerful than the secret weapon of my growing-up years. There was no telling how high I would climb with all this supernatural power at my disposal.

Almost as quickly as I thought of something I wanted, and without my saying a word, people began doing my will. All I had to do was ask, and I had money, women, and success in business. I would never want for anything again. I had found an illimitable pot of gold at the end of an unfading rainbow.

One of my first thoughts, when I realized I could have anything I wanted, was that I shouldn't work for anyone else ever again. I should go back into business for myself. This time, I was bound to prosper.

Almost as soon as I had the thought, Jim Fisk, an attorney whom I knew only casually, just *happened* to drop by my office.

"Sid," he said, "I've been thinking that you just might want to go back into business for yourself. In case you do, I have some extra office space available in my building. We'd be glad to let you have it free—until you get on your feet. We'll supply your phone and secretary. You might even be able to sell some stock in our company, and make some extra commissions for yourself for a starter."

After he left, I thought I'd check with my new power to see what he thought about Fisk's offer.

"Counselor, make me money," I said.

Immediately I was led to open the dictionary at random and point to a word. When I looked down, my finger was on the word "anchor." That was the name of a mutual fund company I had worked with one time in the past. I called them up, and the regional man said they would be delighted for me to open my own office and go into business representing them. Just like that. And just like that, I resigned from my job and set up shop in my free office.

So I resolved to make some study of the Sacred Scriptures and find what kind of books they were. But what I came upon was something not grasped by the proud, not revealed either to children, something utterly humble in the hearing but sublime in the doing, and shrouded deep in mystery. And I was not of the nature to enter into it or bend my neck to follow it. When I first read those Scriptures, I did not feel in the least what I have just said. . . . My conceit was repelled by their simplicity, and I had not the mind to penetrate into their depths. They were indeed of a nature to grow in Your little ones. But I could not bear to be a little one; I was only swollen with pride, but to myself I seemed a very big man.

Chapter 13

The Answer?

At the time I set up my own office, I was ignorant of the fact that Jim Fisk, the president of the computer company that gave me the free space, was a Bible believer. That was bad enough, but even worse, Jim had all the "Jesus people" in town trooping through his offices, and they had prayer meetings morning, noon, and night.

Somehow, although I thought they were all kooks, I liked them. They were more than nice to me, projecting a kind of love and acceptance I had never seen before. And they did it even though they didn't approve of my mind-control involvement. Well, I was glad *they* had that kind of love, but it wasn't for me.

Soon after I had moved into my new free office, I met Art Lane. He was tall, well-built, distinguished-looking with prematurely gray hair, and very articulate. Art had every quality a man of the world ought to have, and I came to admire him greatly. But there was something strange about him. Although Art was a Jew, he attended the Bible studies with the Gentile guys in the office building. I couldn't understand why a Jew would be studying the Scriptures with a bunch of Gentiles. It didn't make sense, but it did arouse my curiosity, so I began attending the sessions, too.

I gave them a hard time, questioning everything they said, ridiculing their faith. But they didn't throw me out. They didn't even give me harsh answers. Gradually it dawned on me that they were praying for me! That made me laugh. It was utterly ridiculous. But if it suited them, let them go ahead. I was glad for my free office and the friendship that gave and gave and gave without requiring anything from me.

One day Art Lane stopped by my office to talk about the insurance business. We talked about other things, too. He told me that he himself had come to "know the Lord" through reading the Hebrew Scriptures and understanding that Yeshua—Jesus—was the One who had fulfilled all the prophecies about the coming Messiah. Then he asked me a question.

"Sid, do you have a Bible?"

"Well, no," I admitted.

"I'll bring you one the next time I drop by," he promised. "But in the meantime—"

Art opened his Bible and showed me some Scriptures telling about the Messiah who was to come, and some additional Scriptures in the New Covenant that showed that a

Jew named Yeshua had fulfilled every single Messianic prophecy.

I was bored with the whole business. "Look, Art," I interrupted, "if the Jewish Messiah had already come, the rabbi in our synagogue would surely have told us all about it—"

"Oh, but that's part of the prophecy, too, Sid," Art smiled. Then he pointed to a verse in the book of the prophet Isaiah, and I read: "He was despised and rejected of men . . . and we esteemed him not."

"You see, Sid," Art went on, "if we Jews had *received* Yeshua the first time He came, He would not have been the Messiah."

With that intriguing remark hanging in the air, Art left my office. But the gleam in his eye warned me that he was in league with the Bible believers who were praying that I would acknowledge this Yeshua as my Messiah and put Him in charge of my life.

Well, they could pray all they wanted. But I was quite satisfied with my own life, thank you. Being separated from my wife, I had freedom to come and go as I pleased, and with my fast-growing mind-control powers, I would soon have the material world on a string. If there *was* a Messiah, I didn't need Him for anything.

Another of the men in the office building who attended the Bible-study/prayer meetings was Gene Griffin. He was an inventor who had spent a year in a kibbutz, a community farm, in Israel. I thought it strange that a Gentile, a goy, would take a year out of his life just to help Israel. And I noticed something else strange about Gene. He didn't act like a businessman or an inventor. It seemed that every time I looked at him, he was reading the Bible.

"You know, Sid," Gene said to me one day, "your God, the God of Abraham, and Isaac, and Jacob, is not pleased with your involvement in mind control. He condemns all occult practices."

"What do you know about my God?" I challenged.

"Plenty," he assured me. "Because there's only one God. My God is the same as your God. And if you'll read the eighteenth chapter of Deuteronomy in your own Tenach, your Jewish Bible, especially the ninth through the twelfth verses, God's opinion about the occult will be plain to you."

I picked up the Bible Art had given me a few days previously, thumbed to Deuteronomy and read:

> When thou art come into the land which the Lord they God giveth thee, thou shalt not learn to do after the abominations of those nations. There shall not be found among you any one that maketh his son or his daughter to pass through the fire, or that useth divination, or an observer of times, or an enchanter, or a sorcerer, or a charmer, or a consulter with familiar spirits, or a wizard, or a necromancer. For all that do these things are an abomination to the Lord . . .

Talk about relevance! The Scripture made it sound as if reading my horoscope, visiting my fortune-teller, and consulting my counselor were things not pleasing to God. They were actually abominations!

"Aw, that can't mean what you think it does," I told Gene, closing the book. "Just like I've been telling you guys, God's in charge of all knowledge. Why, He probably *wants* us to explore every avenue of knowledge— supernatural, natural, the whole bit. Everything we can learn about good *or* evil is to our benefit."

"Ever hear what happened to Adam and Eve when they nibbled at the fruit of the tree of the knowledge of good and evil?" he asked.

"Fer cryin' out loud! How naive can you get!" I exploded. "Don't you guys realize that these things have been handed down and handed down from one generation to the next? There are many difficulties in translating any language; and probably so many errors have crept in the Scriptures that what they say now isn't even remotely related to what the original said."

I didn't realize I had been shouting until Gene answered me in a super-soft voice, telling me that God had protected the authenticity of the Bible in supernatural ways. But I wasn't buying any of that.

The next afternoon, I was trying to talk Jim Fisk into digging into his subconscious mind through mind control. Apparently he had had more than enough of my hassling because after a while, he put his hands over his ears. When I took the hint and shut up, he let me have it.

"Look, Sid. I don't want to talk to you anymore about it. I don't want to argue with you. I can't handle it. Tell you what you can do. You won't take my word for anything, you won't take the Bible's word for anything. So okay. But why don't you ask God who Jesus is?" With that, he strode out of the office.

I hadn't told Jim I would ask God about that, but it was an interesting question to think about. I wondered what God would tell me if did I ask Him. But God had never told me anything before. And I wasn't in the habit of asking Him anything.

"Look," I told myself, "I'll accept that this Jesus was a man, a real historic figure. And He probably was a good teacher, lived a moral and upright life—

"But if that's all He was," I interrupted myself, "why are people so all-fired excited about Him two thousand years later, just as if He's still alive?"

That was another interesting question. But it hung in the air, unanswered and unanswerable.

At that moment, I happened to notice a little white leaflet parked on the corner of my desk. Jim Fisk had handed it to me one day. I had flipped through without reading it, and had put it down on my desk where it had rested, undisturbed. For some reason, I picked up the leaflet now, and began reading.

"Have you heard of the four spiritual laws?" the cover asked. I hadn't, so I read on.

The leaflet was simple, easy to read. The first law said that God loved me and that He had a plan for my life. Well, that was all right. I had a plan for my life, too; I wanted to be famous and rich. God's plan couldn't beat that.

The second law said that man is sinful and separated from God. That was probably true, too, but so what? Then the third law said that Jesus, Yeshua in Hebrew, was God's remedy for man's sin and separation from Him. The fourth law said that in order for a man to have this remedy, he had to "receive Jesus . . . by personal invitation."

Each of the spiritual laws was supported by quotations from the New Testament. After the four spiritual laws had been explained, there was a page with a prayer on it that a person could pray to invite this Jesus into his heart.

I wasn't really interested in doing that, but I figured it couldn't hurt anything, so just sitting there in my chair, I read the prayer aloud, very softly so that if anyone happened to come in, they wouldn't know what I was up to:

> Lord Jesus, forgive my sins. I open the door of my life
> and receive you as my Savior and Lord. Take control of

the throne of my life. Make me the kind of person you
want me to be. Thank you for coming into my life and for
hearing my prayer as you promised.

That was all there was to it. When I had finished reading the prayer, I didn't feel any different. No lights flashed,
I didn't hear anything. And I figured the prayer hadn't
"worked." Well, that was perfectly all right with me. I had
just read it for kicks anyway. I had known all along that
there wasn't anything to all this Jesus business, and now I
was satisfied that I had proved it.

At quitting time that afternoon, Gene Griffin stuck his
head in the door, breaking into my thoughts with a startling
question.

"Sid, if God says that all who dabble in the occult are
an abomination to Him, guess where your supernatural
power is coming from."

Gene just stood there, waiting for my answer. But I
didn't have one! Where *was* the power coming from?

Fear hit me for a split second. Was there a devil?
Could I be in league with him? Could the devil be the
source of my power in mind control?

It couldn't be. That bit about the devil was just
superstitious nonsense. I snapped back to my senses.

"Look, Gene. Like I told you. I don't believe the Bible
we have today is the Bible God wrote originally. Man has
changed it over the centuries. And there probably isn't
such a thing as the devil."

Gene didn't answer. He just smiled and slipped
quietly from my office, leaving me to argue with myself.

Even though I didn't understand all of that
Deuteronomy scripture, and I wasn't sure the Bible was
the word of God, the thought that I might be in league with

the devil was planted in my mind, and it began to grow.

I decided to get the answer from the mind-control people themselves. I would ask them where the power was coming from. They would know.

That night I went to see my local instructor.

"Bill, just where does this power we use in mind control come from?"

"Search me, Sid," he said. "I don't know. I've never given it any thought, actually."

He didn't know! The man who had tapped me into my counselor didn't know where the power came from!

Bill saw the fear in my face.

"Sid, maybe you'd better not take the advanced course," he suggested. "I'll refund your money But if you really want an answer to your question, I'll arrange a meeting for you with the top instructor in mind control in the country."

I jumped at the offer. The meeting was scheduled for two weeks from that day, in Harrisburg, Pennsylvania.

I could hardly wait to tell Gene about it. "You and your friends and your Bible can go with me to Harrisburg," I said, planning it all out in my mind. "You can sit on one side of the table and the mind-control man on the other. I'll sit in the middle, and may the best power win."

But Gene said he'd have to pray about it first, and after he had prayed, he told me that God didn't want him to go to the meeting with me. I exploded. That messed up my beautiful plan, and when the day came, I found myself on the road to Harrisburg, feeling more foolish with every passing mile. I felt as if I was taking the trip to defend the Bible, a book I didn't even believe in.

When I was seated across a luncheon table from the instructor, we talked about everything except the burning subject until the waitress brought our dessert. I began by asking, "What do you think of evil?"

He laughed at the foolishness of my question before he dismissed it with an unequivocal answer, "There's no such thing as evil." He was so cocksure, I knew he had to be right. How humiliating it would be to argue with someone who spoke with such authority.

Almost apologetically, I showed him the Bible and asked him what he thought about it. He smiled and said, "It's a good book, but there are lots of good books." His manner suggested that any fool would know that.

To my great relief, before I could ask him anything else, he called for his check and said he had to be going. His parting remark was, "By the way, Mr. Roth, the next time you want to ask me something, no need to drive all these miles to do it. Don't pick up your telephone either. Just address your thoughts to me, and I'll pick them up and send your answers back, mind to mind. Cheaper than postage, you know, and a whole lot faster service." He slid a tip under the edge of his plate, strode to the cash register and then out of the restaurant.

I just sat there with my mouth hanging open. Boy! Think of how tremendous *his* powers were. Just wait until mine were that developed!

Mind control was really the thing. I would stop listening to my kooky religious friends who were trying to scare me out of using it. They could stay back in the boondocks if they wanted. I would get ahead with *my* life.

Your wrath had grown mighty against me and I knew it not. I had grown deaf from the clanking of the chain of my mortality, the punishment for the pride of my soul: and I departed further from You, and You left me to myself: and I was tossed about and wasted and poured out and boiling over in my fornications. . . . You were silent, and I, arrogant and depressed, weary and restless, wandered further and further from You into more and more sins which could bear no fruit save sorrows.

Chapter 14

Seed of Fear

At the next mind-control meeting I attended, someone told me that a friend of his had used his mind-control powers on a jockey at a horse race, causing him to fall from his horse, and nearly get killed. The accident let the mind-control guy's nag win the race! *Wow, that's power*, I thought.

But some long-dormant vestige of conscience in me bristled at the thought that mind-control power could be used to hurt somebody. I had been told it could only be used for good.

At the same meeting, some of the more advanced students were asking their counselors what they would be doing in the future. I asked the most advanced student what his counselor saw me doing a year from now.

"Just a minute, Sid, and I'll find out," he said. He closed his eyes, lowered his brain waves, and almost immediately his eyes flew open. There was a startled look on his face.

"Sid, I don't understand. My counselor has always been a perfect gentleman with me, but when I asked him what you would be doing a year from today, he started cursing and using all kinds of vulgarity. And he refused to answer my question."

The instructor had no explanation for this strange kind of behavior from a counselor. He'd never encountered such a thing before, he said. What was wrong? Did the counselor see something so horrible he couldn't mention it? The seed of fear in me began to sprout and push upward.

At another meeting, a few days later, the whole class went into deep meditation. Something new happened! I saw myself come out of myself!

I was so excited, I came out of my meditation and breathlessly told the woman next to me about it.

"Oh, Sid," she said, "I'm so happy for you! You have just found your astral soul. Now you can *really* have everything you want, greater power than you ever dreamed."

For a few moments, I sat there, quietly exulting in the fact that nothing would be beyond my reach. But then I felt her hand on my arm.

"But Sid, let me warn you about something. Never let your astral soul take you too far from your body. You might not be able to find your way back."

"Not be able to find my way back?" I could feel the gooseflesh rising on my arms. "But that would mean—that would mean—I'd be dead—if my body was in one place and my soul in another—" I stammered. She nodded gravely, closed her eyes, and went back into her meditative state.

The seed of fear that had sprouted was growing in me. I shoved it down, rubbed my arms to make the gooseflesh go away, and resolved to be careful not to go too far from my body. The sensible thing was to keep my body in full view at all times. That way, I could always find my way back. Satisfied that such a precaution would be sufficient to prevent anything bad from happening to me, I continued to exercise my powers.

At a mind-control meeting the next week, the subject of astral projection came up again. The instructor explained that every time we sleep, our astral soul goes for a walk.

I nearly fell out of my chair. The pricklings of fright were chilling my flesh again. When I was awake, I could control my comings and goings, but how could I do so when I was asleep?

I shook my head, trying to clear it of my gruesome imaginings. After all, I wasn't asleep. I *was* awake. I was in *perfect* control of myself.

The next morning at the office, I had an urge to do my dictionary trick again, this time without asking a specific question in advance. I opened the book, wrote down the first word my finger pointed to, closed the book, opened it at random again, and continued the process until I had five words written on a piece of paper. I did a double take when I realized that they made a sentence: "Refrain from this sinful dictionary."

Where was *that* advice coming from? I crumpled the paper, flung it in the wastebasket, and pretended to return to the work on my desk. But the disquiet inside me wouldn't settle down, wouldn't be still. I was seething with some kind of spiritual distress, something I had never felt before.

When Gene walked into my office a few minutes later, I told him what had happened, and how I was feeling. To my surprise, he didn't try to comfort me, he just threw his hands into the air and began to laugh and praise God for His goodness. That didn't make me feel any better. Next, Jim Fisk walked in to see what all the racket was about. When Gene told him, Jim looked long and hard at me and said, "Sid, you look like you have a bad case of spiritual neurosis." Then he winked at Gene, and made a victory sign, saying, "Looks like Sid's about ready for his breakdown, huh?"

Jim was obviously needling me. What were they doing? Were they trying to crowd me into some kind of hysteria or something?

For a moment there flashed through my mind the treatment I had given Chuck Hoffman way back in "Hootenanny" days, and for the first time, I felt an uncomfortable flood of remorse about what I had done to him.

The office was getting unbearable for me. I had to get out, so I threw some papers in a briefcase and got out as fast as I could.

Could it be that my Bible-believing friends were right? Was there really a devil? By my involvement in the occult, had I cast my lot with him?

*And You sent Your hand from above, and raised my
soul out of that depth of darkness. . . .*

Chapter 15

Out of the Pit

As I backed my car out of the parking area, I kept getting flashes of incidents in my past, all ugly ones.

My childhood tantrum on the train, racing around the table to get away from my father, copping out on my paper route, tattling, lying, cheating in school, refusing to staple letters together, leaving snarls of improperly done work behind me in more job changes than I could count, always trying to get something for nothing, profiting at the other fellow's expense, being unfaithful to Joy and thinking I was so smart to get by with it . . .

That was the afternoon of increasing terror. That was the night I went to bed with the mezuzah around my neck, the Bible under my pillow, fear enveloping me, and a broken heart inside me. That was the night I prayed to the God of Abraham, Isaac, and Jacob and asked Him to help me. That was the night I asked Joy to entreat *her* God in my behalf.

The next thing I knew, it was morning. Sunshine streamed through my window and woke me up. I was alive, really alive. The fear was gone, completely gone, and in its place was an indescribable joy. It was as if I had died in my sleep, and had wakened, brand-new, in a brand-new world.

And I wasn't alone. Someone was with me. It was Yeshua, the Messiah of Israel. He had made the perfect atonement for all my sins, and I didn't have to feel guilty anymore.

It was almost too much for me to grasp. The door I had opened in ignorarce was closed, not behind me, shutting me into evil forever, but before me, as if I had never opened it.

That morning, my life began all over again. It was just as God had promised:

> I will make a new covenant with the house of Israel, and with the house of Judah: Not according to the covenant that I made with their fathers . . . which . . . they broke . . .: I will put my law in their inward parts, and write it in their hearts; and will be their God, and they shall be my people. For I will forgive their iniquity, and I will remember their sin no more (Jeremiah 31:30-33).

As I accepted that forgiveness for myself, I understood what Jim and Gene and Art had been trying to tell me. They had been just words before, words I had hardly believed, but now they were made alive in me.

The altar at Jerusalem had been destroyed in A.D. 70, along with the Temple, so the high priest could no longer enter the Holy of Holies every year, to sprinkle the blood of animals securing the forgiveness of sins committed during the year that had passed. But God had provided a new sacrificial lamb. The blood of Yeshua Ha'Mashiach, Jesus the Messiah, was the perfect once-for-all atonement.

As I drove to the office, brimming with eagerness to share what had happened to me, my heart was singing. There *was* something more. God Himself had come to live within me.

That morning, I had an appointment with Don Tobias, a Gentile believer. I was trying to interest him in investing in Jim Fisk's company, but we didn't talk business very long. Don was God-sent; he was able to explain some things to me that I had not understood.

After we had talked and prayed together for nearly an hour, Don went down the hall to meet with Jim Fisk and Gene Griffin. The next thing I knew, both of them were in my office.

"Sid, Don's just told us of your commitment to Yeshua! Congratulations!" Gene's eyes sparkled and his face was lit with joy as he said it.

A few tears escaped Jim Fisk's eyes as he strode over to shake my hand in both of his.

"Welcome, Sid, welcome," he choked out, too full for any more words. And I knew that after all my years of searching down the wrong paths for the wrong things, I had finally arrived at the place God had prepared for me before the beginning of time.

O Lord God, grant us peace, for Thou has granted us all things, the peace of repose, the peace of Thy Sabbath, the peace that has no evening. For this gloriously beautiful order of things that are very good will pass away when it has achieved its end; it will have its morning and its evening.

Chapter 16

A Gracious Life

In the days that followed, I began to read the Bible with new understanding. I was simply amazed at the number of specific Old Covenant prophecies that Yeshua fulfilled.

His virgin birth in Bethlehem, His entrance to Jerusalem, His rejection and execution, His resurrection and ascension—almost every significant aspect of His life had been accurately foreshadowed in the messianic prophecies.*

---

*See Appendix for a list of Old Testament Scriptures fulfilled by Yeshua.

One day, as I was reading the words of the Messiah about marriage, I knew it was His will for me to be reconciled to my wife. We had been seeing one another frequently, and she had sensed a profound change in me. She saw that I was concerned about her, whereas before I had been utterly and unbelievably selfish. Joy told me that during the night when I had been about to die with fear, she had slipped from her bed to say a prayer for the first time in many years.

"God," she had prayed, "if You're there, please help Sid." That was all, but He had heard. And Joy saw that He had answered.

As the weeks rolled by, I became aware of His guiding my every step, just as I had asked Him to do when, without faith, that day in my office, I had read the prayer that invited Him to take charge of me.

Before many days had passed, Joy and I were living together again, and our little daughter, Leigh, had a mother and a father to love her. The things of the world that had had such a stranglehold on my attention no longer interested me. I yearned to know more about God and His plan for my life, and I thanked Him continually for my narrow escape from the forces of darkness to which I had opened my life through my involvement in fortune-telling, horoscopes, and mind control.

I wanted to warn everyone that there are two supernatural powers at work in the world, the supernatural power from God and the other supernatural power, which comes disguised as an angel of light, but is laced through and through with evil. No wonder all occult involvement is an abomination to God. It is Satan's instrument to steal, kill, and destroy the very creatures for whom Yeshua died that they might have eternal life.

Soon, I began to receive invitations to speak to groups all over the country. After telling my story, I would see others who were in occult bondage renounce Satan and invite God to take over their lives. I watched in amazement as I saw God working.

One day, I had the joy of seeing my sister Shirley and her husband, Marc, receive the Messiah as my friend, Don Tobias, led them in prayer. With Marc, however, the new commitment was short-lived. The next morning Marc telephoned me and took it all back.

"Look, Sid, I know that you needed the Messiah, because your life was all messed up. You were separated from Joy and mixed up in the occult and all that. But for me, well, it's different. I must have been hypnotized when I said what I did last night. There was no reason for me to do it. I have everything I need. I'm happy with my wife, have a good job, and I just don't need this in my life."

Before I could offer any arguments, he went on, "I'm going back to the way I was before. I don't need God." Then he hung up.

But Shirley held to her commitment. I was confident that as she lived her new life where Marc could see it, he would reconsider his choice. God would ultimately accomplish His purpose in Marc.

Sooner than we could have guessed, God began to help Marc see how needy he was.

It happened one night about a year after Marc's abortive decision. I had just finished speaking to a group of believers and was standing at the front of the auditorium praying for a woman who had deep problems. Suddenly, I was aware of someone at my elbow, tugging at my coat.

"Sid, there's an urgent phone call for you."

I ran to the telephone across the hall. The voice at the

other end was incoherently sobbing something about a dead baby.

"Oh my God, not Leigh," I blurted, thinking of my own little girl.

"No. It's Cheryl Ann," the voice managed, and I realized I was talking to my sister Shirley. Her baby girl was not quite two years old.

"Marc found her," Shirley choked out. "Pulled her out of the swimming pool. Oh, Sid, the doctors say she's gone. But—when the Messiah was here on earth—" Quavering determination was in her voice now, and an urgent pleading.

"Sid, He brought the dead back to life—Oh, Sid, do you think—would He—?"

"Keep praying, Shirley. Hold on. I'll come."

The folks at the meeting began to pray for Cheryl Ann, while I sped to the hospital where Shirley and Marc were waiting, hope mingled with hopelessness in their tear-swollen eyes.

Cheryl Ann was lying deathly still on a white-sheeted bed. A futile mechanical respirator was shoved into a corner. I thought, "If God performs this miracle, my whole family will become believers."

But I was about to learn that God doesn't work according to the script we write.

Kneeling beside the bed, my hands on Cheryl Ann's tiny chest, I prayed for a long time. Others came in to join me from time to time—a Protestant minister, a Catholic nun, a black orderly. None of them seemed shocked that I was asking God to raise the baby from the dead.

Suddenly I heard a little sound that was not my own voice nor that of any of the other prayers. Opening my eyes, I saw bubbles coming from Cheryl Ann's nostrils!

"She's alive!" I shouted, and ran to the hallway to get the nurse who had just left the room.

"I'm sorry," she said, returning to the room with me. "Those bubbles don't mean that she's alive. That often happens when someone has drowned. It's just carbon dioxide coming out of the lungs."

The nurse went out again. I prayed a little while longer, and gradually I felt the peace of God replace my anguished striving. I bent to kiss Cheryl good-bye, and thanked God that He had remained in charge and that my little niece was safe in His arms.

The next morning, Shirley called to say, "Sid, I can cope with this because of Yeshua. But Marc is almost out of his mind. He can't stand it. He's going to pieces."

As I drove to their house, I praised God for the peace He had given Shirley, and I prayed that Marc would have it too.

When I arrived, two neighbors who were in the living room with Marc left almost immediately. Marc had been struggling to keep his composure, but as soon as they were out the door, he gave way to racking sobs. I had asked God to help me say the right words, but I didn't have to say anything. I waited, praying softly, and Marc finally gathered his voice to speak. It came in an urgent whisper.

"Sid, I need help. Would your Yeshua help me?"

I nodded, and we went to his bedroom where he knelt alongside the bed and surrendered to Yeshua.

"Oh, Sid!" he exclaimed, his eyes widening, his hand spread on his chest. "It's like all the hard, heavy weight has been lifted from my heart! The pain and all that agony. It's gone! I feel something. It's—it's like a cloud of love all over me!"

We began to laugh, with joy.

"It's the Lord, Marc," I said, and he knew I spoke the truth.

Shirley had a new husband. I had a new brother. God had a new son.

At the funeral the next day, all their relatives were astounded at how well Shirley and Marc were taking the tragedy. Uncle Sol came up to me, shaking his head.

"Sid," he said, "I can't get over it—how brave they are. Shirley and Marc are putting up such a front, acting so strong for the family."

"It's not a front, Uncle Sol," I told him. "It's real. Their strength comes from the Messiah who lives inside them."

He looked at me, tears streaming, and shook his head as if he thought I was crazy. I didn't say anything more, but I knew that a seed had been planted.

Cheryl's four-year-old brother, Brian, summed up a lot of things when he said to his mother, "Mommy, now that Cheryl is in heaven, we're bigger, aren't we?"

"No," Shirley said, getting down on her knees to hug him, not understanding what he meant. "You mean we're smaller. We have a smaller family now."

"No, Mommy," Brian persisted, his dark eyes searching the depths of hers. "We're bigger because we all have God inside of us."

One week later, Marc and Shirley accompanied Joy and me to a Kathryn Kuhlman service in Pittsburgh, and Marc gave his testimony before a large congregation in the auditorium as well as to a huge television audience:

> I'm Jewish. I was raised in a Jewish home. We believed in God, and hoped that the Messiah would come some-

day. . . . But just last week, our twenty-one-month-old daughter, Cheryl Ann, was drowned in the swimming pool in our own backyard.

We had always thought she was an angel, sent from heaven. She gave joy to so many people.

It was hard, so hard that I couldn't wait any longer for a Messiah who might come sometime in the future. I needed a Messiah now. And in my great need, my eyes were opened to the truth that the Messiah Yeshua, the Lord Jesus, had already come, fulfilling all the prophecies in the Hebrew Scriptures.

I invited that Messiah to come into my heart, and He did, lifting the burden of sorrow that was too great for me to bear. . . .

What some people look on as a senseless tragedy, my wife and I are able to see as a sign of God's love toward us. Through this, He brought me to Himself. God gave us Cheryl Ann—her name means "gracious life" in Hebrew—to open the gates to everlasting life for our whole family.

Cheryl Ann will be waiting for us in eternity. . . .

When Marc had finished talking, a great throng of people rose from their seats and came to the front of the auditorium. Their eyes had been opened, too, and they wanted to invite the Messiah to take over their lives.

What man will give another man the understanding of this, or what angel will give another angel, or what angel will give a man? Of You we must ask, in You we must seek, at You we must knock. Thus only shall we receive, thus shall we find, thus will it be opened to us.

Chapter 17

Joy in the Morning

With so many wonderful things going on all around us, I thought my wife would surely become a real believer. But somehow, it wasn't working out that way. I was so busy with my business, with speaking engagements all over the country, accelerated by several television appearances, that I was blind to how Joy was receiving it all. I wasn't even aware that I was leaving her and Leigh alone night after night until God used her to open my eyes.

One night I didn't get home until well after midnight. I tiptoed in, expecting to find Joy asleep. But she was sitting up in bed, waiting for me.

The confrontation began softly, but it didn't stay that way.

"Sidney!" she said, in a tone of voice I hadn't heard for a long time, "do you have any idea what time it is? Do you realize that you've been gone every single weekend for a month, plus two or three nights during the week? You know how much I hate to be alone all the time! It's almost like being separated again!"

"But Joy, you know all this is for the Lord!" Was there something more than a hint of self-righteousness in my defense?

"For the Lord?" she screamed. "I thought the Lord said that husbands were to *love* their wives, not to leave them all the time. You call that love?"

I kept trying to defend myself, she kept whacking at my defenses, getting louder and more shrill.

"Shhh! You'll wake up Leigh," I cautioned, trying to calm her, but that just made her madder than ever. In her exasperation, she picked up her pillow and started hitting me with it. Other things began flying through the air, and when a book from her bedside table narrowly missed my head, I finally heard, really heard, what she was saying: I could not serve God to the neglect of my family. I began to recognize how much my ego fed on my popularity and importance with all those needy people at all those meetings. But I was needy, too—I needed to grow up.

In the meantime, some of the girls who worked with Joy in her office were becoming believers, and were bombarding her with their testimonies. They only compounded her defensiveness.

It was about this time that we signed up to go on a tour of Israel. Joy was all for it at first, because she loved to travel, and neither of us had been overseas before.

Almost all of the 150 people on the tour were real Jesus fanatics—except Joy. She became utterly exhausted by so many people talking to her about Jesus all the time. Instead of blessing her, all the talk came through as condemnation, and naturally, she blamed me.

I hadn't yet learned that it is the Holy Spirit of God who draws people to Himself, and that our crowding over-exuberance stood squarely in the way of His work.

One day Joy, sick of the whole tour group, especially me, left us to do some sightseeing on her own. Her cab driver, a displaced Jew who spoke English with a heavy New York accent, was glad enough to take Joy to see the Kennedy shrine, the museum of the six million Jews annihilated during the Second World War, and anything that had to do with the Old Covenant. But she had a hard time persuading him to take her to see anything that had to do with Yeshua.

When, late in the afternoon, she finally persuaded him to take her to the Garden Tomb, the gates had been closed.

"That really hit me," Joy was to tell me later. "It was almost as if God was telling me that if I kept on locking my heart against the Messiah, He would lock His heart against me."

God used the cab driver's resistance to the things of the Messiah, and then the locked gate, to stir Joy's heart where all our pushing had failed. Joy gave her life to Yeshua one morning soon after we returned to the United States. Not long afterward, her mother and father saw the unmistakable change in both of us, and began to worship regularly with us at Beth Messiah Synagogue.

The wooden plaque that hangs in the living room of our home has a double meaning for all of us. It reads:

Joy is the greatest evidence of the presence of God.

For then also You will rest in us, as now You operate in us, so that it will then be Your rest in us as it is now Your work in us. But You, Lord, are ever in action and ever at rest. You do not see in time nor move in time nor rest in time. Yet you make the things we see in time, and You make both time while time is and rest when time is no more.

Chapter 18

Life in Death

I had thought that one could not remain a Jew after receiving the Messiah Yeshua, but knowing Him made me more Jewish than ever. The rituals that had been without meaning for me as a boy began to have life.

I noticed it especially when I began attending the synagogue with my father on all the Jewish holidays. I knew it pleased him, and it was one way I could show him love.

On Yom Kippur, the highest Jewish Holy Day of the year, when Jews pray that God will forgive their sins of the past year and give them life for the New Year, I was sitting beside my Uncle Sol in the synagogue. He was angry at my stand for Yeshua, but he still loved me, he said, and hoped I'd soon come to my senses. I had been praying that God would bring him to the point where he would receive the Messiah, too.

Soon after Yom Kippur, mom, who was working part-time in Uncle Sol's watch repair business, began to notice that something was wrong with him. His lip hung slack on one side, almost as if he had had a stroke, and saliva would run from the corners of his mouth without his being aware of it. His confident stride had changed to a strange sort of shuffle. After several weeks of nagging, the family persuaded him to go to see a doctor.

The diagnosis? A tumor on the brain, in a location that made it inoperable. Uncle Sol would die, and soon, unless chemotherapy was effective in stopping the growth of the malignancy. The doctors were not optimistic about his chances.

Visiting my uncle frequently in the hospital, praying every day for his recovery, even after the doctors conceded that the chemotherapy wasn't working, I watched him shrink from a robust, healthy two-hundred pounds down to a hundred-pound skeleton with skin draped over it. He was fast becoming a vegetable before my eyes, and I knew that, short of a real miracle, he would soon be gone.

"Uncle Sol," I asked him one day, my heart in my mouth with yearning for him, "is it all right if I read to you from the Jewish Bible?"

He was paralyzed with weakness, could not speak at all, but he managed a slight affirmative nod with his head. His sad eyes held the love for me that hadn't stopped through the years.

"O God, give me the right Scriptures," I prayed, as

fervently as I knew how. I began reading the fourteenth psalm:

> The fool hath said in his heart, there is no God. . . .
> There is none that doeth good, no, not one (Psalm 14:
> 1-3).

The deadness of sorrow in his eyes seemed to agree that it was so. I moved on to Isaiah and read,

> Behold, the Lord's hand is not shortened, that it cannot
> save; neither his ear heavy, that it cannot hear; But your
> iniquities have separated between you and your God,
> and your sins have hid his face from you, that he will not
> hear (Isaiah 59:1).

"We have all sinned, Uncle Sol," I said. "We are condemned, unless atonement is made for us. God made provision for our atonement when He commanded the priests, the sons of Aaron, to sacrifice animals and sprinkle their blood around the altar by the door of the tabernacle."

I knew my uncle's Jewish upbringing had acquainted him with all these things.

"But since A.D. 70," I went on, "when the Temple was destroyed along with the genealogies that identified the sons of Aaron, that atonement can't work for us."

The discouragement in his eyes looked impenetrable.

"But there's good news for us, Uncle Sol," I hurried on. "The prophet Jeremiah tells us about it." I turned in the Hebrew Scriptures and read,

> Behold, the days come, saith the Lord, that I will make a
> new covenant with the house of Israel and with the
> house of Judah; Not according to the covenant that I
> made with their fathers in the day that I took them by

> the hand to bring them out of the land of Egypt; which
> my covenant they broke, although I was a lord over
> them, saith the Lord: But this shall be the covenant that
> I will make with the house of Israel; after those days,
> saith the Lord, I will put my law in their inward parts,
> and write it in their hearts; and will be their God, and
> they shall be my people. . . . For I will forgive their in-
> iquity, and I will remember their sin no more (Jeremiah
> 31:30-33).

"That's what happened to me, Sol," I explained. "In
the Old Covenant, an unblemished lamb had to be sac-
rificed, over and over again. But in the New Covenant,
God's Messiah, Yeshua, the Lamb of God, shed His blood
to atone for us forever. Our own prophets spoke about
Him, thousands of years before He came. They told us
exactly where He would be born, and what men would do
to Him, how He would die and be raised from the dead."

My uncle's face was expressionless. It was impossible
to know what he was thinking. But as I began to read other
verses from the prophets and to tell him about their unmistakable fulfillment in Yeshua, a spark of hope was kindled
and seemed to peer out of the deadness in him.

"Uncle Sol," I told him, "David said, 'The stone which
the builders refused is become the head stone of the
corner' (Psalm 118:22). David and Isaiah both prophesied
that our Messiah would never win a popularity contest. If
the Jewish people had accepted Yeshua the first time He
came, He couldn't have been the Messiah. But He will
come back again to defeat the enemies of Israel and to set
up His kingdom of peace. And when He comes the second
time, every one will know who He is."

I could tell he was weighing my words now, and I read
on,

> Surely he hath borne griefs inflicted by us, and suffered
> sorrows we have caused; yet we did esteem him stricken,
> smitten of God, and afflicted. But he was wounded
> through our transgressions, bruised through our in-
> iquities: the chastisement of our peace was upon him,
> and with his wounds we were healed. All we like sheep
> have gone astray: we have turned every one to his own
> way: and the Lord hath caused the iniquity of us all to fall
> upon him (Isaiah 53:4-6).

"Uncle Sol, the Messiah just *has* to have come already.
The prophet Daniel says, in chapter 9, verse 26, that the
Messiah would be cut off, would be killed, and that *afterward*, the Temple would be destroyed. Since the Temple
was destroyed in A.D. 70, it was Yeshua Ha'Mashiach who
fulfilled all these things.

"Oh, Uncle Sol," I pleaded, my voice breaking with
emotion, "wouldn't you like to ask this Messiah into your
heart and life right now? Wouldn't you like for His atoning
blood to wash away your sins and make you ready to live
forever with God?"

Two miracles occurred before my eyes.

My uncle summoned his strength to nod his head yes,
and as I prayed aloud, his voice, which had been gone for
weeks, came back to enable him to pray aloud after me,

> Messiah Yeshua, please forgive me for every sin I've
> ever committed. I'm really sorry for them. Cover them
> with Your blood of atonement, so it will be as if I've
> never sinned. Please come into my heart and take over
> my life.

He said the words, all of them, softly but distinctly,
tears of joy trickling from the corners of his eyes. Before the
prayer, he had no voice, and after he finished the prayer,

he had no voice. We both knew that God had worked a miracle.

Whenever I visited my uncle in the hospital after that, I read the Bible to him. The peace and light on his face continued to grow, even as his physical condition went steadily downhill.

At his funeral, there was no room for grief in the midst of my joy that he had *heard* the words of the Tenach about the Messiah. God promised that His word never returns void but always accomplishes its purposes. And because His promises are Yea and Amen in Yeshua Ha'Mashiach, I had an unshakable certainty that *all* my people would someday receive Him, that all Israel would be saved.

For additional information
or to have questions answered write:
SID ROTH
THE MESSIANIC VISION
BOX 34444
WASHINGTON D.C. 20034

Appendix

Old Covenant Prophecies
Concerning Yeshua And New Covenant Fulfilment*

The seed of the woman—Gen. 3:15 (Rom. 16:20; Gal. 4:4).

He should be of the seed of Abraham—Gen. 12:3; 22:18; 26:4; 28:14 (Mt. 1:1; Lu. 1:54, 55; Acts 3:25; Rom. 4:13; Gal. 3:8).

He should be the seed of Isaac—Gen. 17:1?; 26:2-5 (Rom. 9:6-8; Heb. 11:18).

Judah should be in the line of descent—Gen. 49:10; Ps. 60:7 (Mt. 1:2).

This promise was made to David—II Sam. 7:11, 12, 27; Ps. 89:3, 4, 35-37; Is. 9:6; 55:3, 4; Amos 9:11, 12 (Mt. 1:1; Lu. 1:32, 69; Acts 15:15-18); Ps. 16:8-10 (Acts 2:25-28; 13:34-37).

Messiah was the prophet that was to come—Deut. 18:15, 18, 19 (John 1:45; Acts 3:22, 23; 7:37).

He was to be born in Bethlehem in Judea—Mic. 5:2 (Mt. 2:6; John 7:42; Heb. 7:14).

He was to be born of a virgin—Is. 7:14 (Mt. 1:18-25, Lu. 1:26-38).

The time when He should come and the time of His kingdom was told to Daniel by the angel Gabriel—Dan. 9:22-27 (Mk. 1:15; Lu. 3:15).

He should be brought forth out of Egypt—Hos. 11:1 (Mt. 2:14, 15).

A harbinger should precede Him in His ministry, and make ready a people prepared for Him and His kingdom—Is. 40:3-5 (John 1:19-25).

While John was not the person of Elijah risen from the dead, he was the Elijah that was to come—Mal. 3:1; 4:5, 6 (Mt. 11:14; 17:9-13; Mk. 9:13; Lu. 1:15-17, 76, 77; 7:37).

Death of the innocents—Jer. 31:15 (Mt. 2:16-18).

He was favored by God and men—Is. 40:5 (Lu. 2:40).

He was to lead the people as the faithful shepherd—Is. 11:1-9; 42:1-4 (John 10:11-18).

He was to be the liberator of the race—Is. 61:1-3 (Lu. 4:16-22; Heb. 2:8-10).

He would live at Capernaum and give light to the land of Zebu lun and Naphtali—Is. 9:1, 2 (Mt. 4:12-16).

He should be a healer of many—Is. 53:4 (Mt. 8:14-17; Acts 10:37-39).

The deaf should hear and the blind see—Is. 29:18, 19; 35:3-6; 42:5-8 (Mt. 11:2-6; Lu. 7:22).

To be known and to save by his knowledge—Is. 53:11 (John 4:39-42).

He taught by the use of parables—Ps. 49:4; 78:2 (Mt. 13:1-53).

He did not lift up His voice in the streets—Is. 42:2.

His whole life attests the truth of the statement, "He was the prince of peace"—Is. 9:6 (Eph. 2:14).

His zeal for the house of God greatly endangered Him—Ps. 69:9; 119:139; Is. 56:7; Jer. 7:11 (Mt. 21:13; Lu. 19:46; John 2:17).

His triumphal entry into Jerusalem—Zech. 9:9 (John 12:12-16).

Taught the resurrection from the dead—Is. 26:19; Ez. 37:1-8; Dan. 12:1-4 (Mk. 12:18-27; John 5:28, 29).

In this way was his death foretold—Mt. 12:38-40; Mk. 8:31-33; 9:9, 10; 10:32-34; John 12:31-34; 20:6-10.

As a shepherd of the flock He should be smitten and spat upon, and the sheep should be scattered—Mic. 5:1; Is. 50:6; Zech. 13:7 (Mt. 26:31, 67).

He was rejected by His own people—Is. 53:1, 3 (John 1:11, 12).

He was silent before His accusers—Is. 53:7 (Mt. 27:12-14; Mk. 15:3-4; Lu. 23:8-10).

He confounds His questioners—Is. 52:13-15 (Mt. 22:34-40).

Herod and Pilate become friends to crucify Him—Ps. 2:1-5 (Acts 4:25-28).

He was betrayed for thirty pieces of silver—Ps. 41:9; 55:12-21; Zech. 11:12, 13 (Mt. 26:14-16, 23, 48-50; 27:3-10; John 13:18-30).

The trials—Ps. 27:12; Is. 53:7 (Mk. 14:53-64).

He was maltreated—Ps. 35:15; Is. 50:5, 6 (John 19:1-6).

They gave Him gall and vinegar—Ps. 69:21 (Mt. 27:34, 35, 48).

They crucified Him—Ps. 22:16; Zech. 12:10, 11 (Lu. 23:33; John 19:37).

He was put to death between thieves—Is. 53:8, 9, 12. (Lu. 22:37).

They cast lots for His vesture—Ps. 22:17, 18 (Mt. 27:35).

The rabble railed on Him—Ps. 22:7, 8, 11; 35:16-22 (Mk. 15:29-32).

He suffered alone—Ps. 22:1; 53:3, 4; Is. 63:1-6 (Mt. 27:45-47).

His committal of His spirit—Ps. 31:5 (Lu. 23:46).

A bone of Him should not be broken—Ps. 34:20 (John 19: 31-37).

He made intercession for the transgressors—Is. 53:12 (Lu. 23:34).

He was with the wicked and the rich in death and burial—Is. 53:9 (Mt. 27:57-60; Mk. 15:42-47; Lu. 23:50-53; John 19:34-42).

He rose from the dead—Ps. 16:8-11 (John 20:1-10; Acts 2:25-32; 13:35-37; 17:2, 3; I Cor. 15:1-7).

He died that our sins might be forgiven—Is. 53:4, 5, 6, 10, 11 (Mt. 20:28; 26:28; Heb. 9:26-28; I Pet. 3:18).

He conquered death for us—Hos. 13:14 (I Cor. 15:20-23).

Messiah ascended up into heaven—Ps. 24·7-10; 68:18; Dan. 7:13, 14 (Eph. 4:9-11).

He was the stone that was rejected and yet made the head of the corner—Ps. 118:22; Is. 28:16 (Mt. 21:42; Mk. 12:10, 11; Lu. 20:17; Acts 4:11).

He became priest and king upon his throne—Gen. 49:10; Ps. 2:6; 110:4; 132:11; Is. 2:4; 9:6, 7; 32:1; Zech. 6:13 (Mt. 22:44, 45; Mk. 12:35-37; Lu. 20:40-43; Acts 2:30; Heb. 4:14, 15; 7:17; 9:24).

His kingdom is an everlasting kingdom—II Sam. 7:12, 13; Ps. 45:6, 7; 89:3, 4, 29-37; Dan. 2:44· Mic. 4:7 (Mk. 1:14, 15; Col. 1:13; Rev. 1:9).

Thus He swallowed up death in victory—Ps. 16:8-10; Is. 25:8; Hos. 13:14 (John 5:28, 29; 11:25, 26; Acts 2:24-28; Rom. 5:21; 6:9; I Cor. 15:21, 54, 55; Eph. 4:8-10; Col. 2:15; Heb. 2:9, 14, 15; Rev. 1:18; 20:13, 14; 21:4).

Having ascended into heaven, He sent forth the Holy Spirit—Is. 32:15; Joel 2:28-32 (Lu. 24:49; John 14:16, 17, 25, 26; 16:7-14; Acts 1:4, 5; 2:1-4, 16-21).

This was the going forth of the new law of the kingdom—Is. 2:1-3; Jer. 31:31-34; Mic. 2:1, 2 (Acts 2:37-42; Heb. 8:6-13).

The Son of God—Ps. 2:7 (Acts 13:33; Heb. 1:5; 5:5).

The Son of man—Ps. 8:4-6 (I Cor. 15:27, 28). (Jesus calls Himself "Son of man" in over fifty instances).

His sinlessness—Is. 53:9 (John 8:46; I Pet. 2:22).

His innocence and meekness—Is. 53:7, 8 (Acts 8:32-35).

His sacrifice surpasses all others—Ps. 40:6-8 (Heb. 10:5-14).

---

*List adapted from Logos Study Bible.